Clydesdales

The World's Most Magical Horse

Mark Shaw

Copyright© 2005, Great American Publishing Company, c/o Great American Mercantile, 9458 West SR 120, Orland, Indiana 46776

All rights reserved. No part of this book shall be reproduced in any form by any means, electronic or mechanical, including photocopying, recording, or by any information storage or retrieval system, without written permission of the publisher. Although every preparation has been taken in the completion of this book, the publisher and author assumes no responsibility for errors or omissions. No liability is assumed for damages resulting from the use of the information contained herein.

Publisher's Cataloging—In—Publication Data

Mark Shaw 1945—

Clydesdales, The World's Most Magical Horse

p. cm.

ISBN 0-9770447-0-X

1. Shaw, Mark 1945— .

2. Clydesdales

3. Horses

4. Heavy Horses

5. I. Shaw, Mark II. Title

10 9 8 7 6 5 4 3 2 1

Printed in the United States of America by Commercial Graphics,

212 Growth Parkway, Angola, Indiana 46706

The World's Most Magical Horse

Dedicated To:

August A. Busch, Jr.,
Whose Belief In Clydesdales Helped Save The Breed

and

Berry Ferrell,
Who So Loved The Clydesdales

Sponsored By:

The Clydesdale Breeders Association of the U.S.A.

With Funding Provided By

Jack and Sue Shaw

Mark Shaw Books

Clydesdales, The World's Most Magical Horse

From Birdies To Bunkers

Book Report

Grammar Report

From Anger to Inspiration

Poetry Report

Writers' Report

Self-Publishing Report

Child of Mercy

Let The Good Times Roll

Code of Silence

Miscarriage of Justice, The Jonathan Pollard Story

Larry Legend

Testament To Courage

Forever Flying

Bury Me In A Pot Bunker

Jack Nicklaus, Golf's Greatest Champion

The Perfect Yankee

Diamonds In The Rough

Down For The Count

The World's Most Magical Horse

The Clydesdales Horse.

Thudding hoof and flowing hair,
Style and action sweet and fair,
Bone and sinew well-defined,
Movement close, both fore and hind.

Noble eye, and handsome head,
Bold, intelligent, well-bred;
Lovely neck, and shoulder laid,
See how shapely he is made.

Muscle strong, and frame well-knit,
Strength personified and fit;
Thus the Clydesdales—see him go
To the field, the stud, the show!

Proper back, and ribs well-sprung,
Sound of limb, and sound of lung;
Powerful loin, and quarter wide,
Grace and majesty allied.

Basic power—living force—
Equine King—The Clydesdales Horse!"

O. R. Cadian
The Clydesdales Breed
Published by the Clydesdales
Horse Society of Great Britain
& Ireland, 1938

Contents

Author's Note

I.	The Magical Horse	7
II.	The Horse, Of Course	17
III.	The Magnificent Clydesdales	35
IV.	The International Clydesdales	45
V.	The American Clydesdales 1900 - 1940	59
VI.	Saving The Clydesdales	67
VII.	Owning A Clydesdale	89
VIII.	Showing The Clydesdales — Where and How	105
IX.	Horse Yarns — Some May Even Be True	117

Appendix:

- Clydesdale Store Items 128
- Bibliography 129
- Clydesdale Association Contacts 130

Author's Note

For more than one-hundred-and-fifty years, the world has enjoyed a love affair with the wondrous Clydesdales. They are gentle giants possessing many of the same characteristics—a friendly manner, loyalty, good manners, humbleness (despite their overwhelming size), affectionate nature, willingness to help animal and human alike, and a soothing calm—that we admire in many human beings.

For me, learning about their heritage, their history, their evolution through the years, and their continuing popularity has been a true blessing, one that occurred through a series of those "meant to be" experiences we all encounter. Before this occurred, I was an admirer of these majestic creatures, but had little knowledge of where they originated or why it is important for us to chronicle their history.

During the winter of 2003/2004, I had witnessed the celebration of the Budweiser band of Clydesdales when they appeared in the annual Christmas parade in my hometown of Aspen, Colorado. On a cold, snowy day, it was if they had jumped out of a Bud commercial to entertain and delight those who stood along the streets and gazed at their beauty and grace. What wonderful animals, I thought to myself, knowledgeable that my older brother Jack and his wife Sue raised them on their farm in upstate Indiana a few miles from their home in Coldwater, Michigan.

While visiting Jack and Sue in August of 2004, I was driven to their Great American Clydesdales farm with roots stretching back to the dairy-farm days of Sue's parents. Approaching the acreage, I viewed two of the brown-colored beauties basking in the sunshine on a blue sky day with just a wisp of breeze. How pastoral this scene was: a calm contrast to the rest of the world dealing with political problems around the globe.

Entering one of the three large barns on the property, I watched as an attendant cut the facial hair of a huge Clydesdale horse that simply stood there as if he had entered the town barbershop. There was no whining, no upset nature, just a cooperative attitude that I would come to know with each of the mystical horses that roamed the Indiana countryside.

Being a curious fellow, I immediately wanted to know more—what was their orgin, how did they differ from other heavy horses, why did they have such great dispositions, how much did they eat, what was the story behind the fluffy hair that overhung their giant-sized hooves like too-long shaggy pants, and why did they high-step like soldiers in an army instead of simply moving along at a faster pace like others of their horse brethren?

Instead of asking Jack these questions, I simply said, "Has anyone written a recent book about the Clydesdales?" His answer, "Well, I don't know."

A few weeks later, my sister Anne accompanied Jack to the National Clydesdale Show held in tandem with the Wisconsin State Fair. While there, she visited the Clydesdale tent sponsored by the Clydesdale Breeders of the U.S.A. Besides purchasing a few souvenirs, Anne asked about whether a book was available.

Standing behind the counter was Betty Groves and her daughter Cathy Behn, the twin forces behind the association. Cathy said to Anne, "Why no, but if we had a book, we could have sold an awful lot of them today."

Having heard Jack inform her of my interest in a book about the Clydesdales, Anne told him of the conversation with Cathy. Within two weeks, a deal had been struck for me to do what I love best, research a subject I know nothing about and then write a book about it.

Conversations with Cathy triggered an early September visit to the national headquarters of the association. Driving from O'Hare Airport outside Chicago, I zigzagged across an Illinois countryside packed with fields full of seven-foot corn, through Winnebago (not, as I learned, the home of the trailers, but named after Indians of the same name) to the dandy town of Pecatonica.

Learning to pronounce that name took awhile, but soon I was on Kelley road and able to drive to the Groves family farm, home to the association and a group of people that warmed my heart.

For two days, Betty, Cathy, her husband John, sons Ryan and Logan, and Clydesdale expert Jim Emmons, who drove from his home near Galesville, Wisconsin, educated me about the wonderful world of the Clydesdales. What grand tour guides these people were, patient with one who didn't know a Clydesdale from Seabiscuit before taking on the responsibility of writing a book about the former.

Besides being entertained at a Friday night Winnebago Indians-Marengo Indians football game (there are 2,500 people in Winnebago, but there were 10,000 people at the game!) and eating two mouthwatering meals that made me want to move to the "P" city even though I still couldn't pronounce it, I was served up historical books, multiple copies of the *Clydesdale News*, colorful photographs, and a heavy helping of sage information that began to answer all of the questions I had about these magnificent animals.

A special treat occurred when I accompanied Ryan to the barn to see him tend to Renee and Julie, a yearling and a two-year-old. To my amazement, Julie stood still while Ryan yanked off her pie-sized horseshoes, all the while gulping down a heavy dose of hay, oats, and alfalfa grass.

Ryan's gentleness with the Clydesdales was tested when Jackie and Roxie, two youngsters, decided they wanted pasture instead of barn. Later, I would gain a glimpse of Memory, a pretty mare that Ryan's eighteen-month-old daughter Abbey loved enough to call all of their horses "Memory," regardless of their names.

When I departed the Groveses' farm with a suitcase full of Clydesdale books and artifacts, I had enough material for ten books. But most important to that visit was a special camaraderie that I had discovered with the Clydesdales even though I had spent just a few hours with them. Whoever said that there is a special bond between these legendary horses and mankind is right, for to know Clydesdales, even for a few minutes, is to love them.

Upon returning to my home in Aspen, Colorado, colleague Kelly James and I began to organize the incredible amount of research material about the Clydesdales. She became as enthusiastic as I was about the book, and together we began to create a sense of what the Clydesdale story, past and present, would be.

In early October, our research files, especially in the historical sense, blossomed when I traveled to Lanarkshire County, Scotland to see firsthand the birthplace of the horses. Traveling from Paris through the English Channel to London, I embarked on a wondrous motorcar trip through the countryside of England, past Oxford and Stratford-on-Avon, the birthplace of Shakespeare, into Scotland.

When I crossed the border, a fresh chill in the air welcomed me and I could almost hear bagpipes bellowing in the lush green valleys as cattle and sheep roamed freely. Soon the road sign imprinted with Lanark appeared, and my right-hand-drive car veered off the M-74 autobahn along a curvy, narrow road replete with several roundabouts.

When I entered the "burgh" of Lanark, location for the initial meeting of the Scots Parliament in 978, I drove past the ancient Greyfriars Parish Church. A quick right turn placed me on High Street and across the street from St. Nicholas Parish, completed in 1774 and formally a medieval chapel. Embedded in stone below the mystical steeple was a life-sized Robert Forest sculpture of William Wallace, who is said to have defended the freedom of this land in 1297. He was memorialized by actor/producer Mel Gibson in the motion picture, *Braveheart*.

After spending time soaking up the history before me, I drove along Wellgate Head toward

New Lanark, a kilometer south of Lanark, where my stay at the eighteenth century New Lanark Mill Hotel provided the perfect view of the famous River Clyde. The next day I scampered up the moist, dirt path for a first-hand glance at the Falls of Clyde, a massive charge of rushing water spitting into the river, one that had been flowing through the spacious gorge for more than 10,000 years.

Standing on a ledge staring at the falls, the deafening roar before me, I watched as the cascading water, with a brown tone to it, gushed downward to a cresting flat point. Then it splattered some thirty feet into the river with splashes so loud they hurt my ears.

The next day I learned more of the history of the Clydesdale horse through the efforts of three experts: John and Shona Zawadzki and Tom Brewster. At the Zawadzki home, squeezed into a lush valley near Lesmahagow, a village with a history dating back to the twelfth century that is famous for, among other things, being the birthplace of patriot Alexander Muir, author of the song, "The Maple Leaf for Ever," I felt as if I had returned to the old days when Clydesdales were the mainstay of the agricultural scene.

After meeting three gentle Clydesdales (dam Quaker Cherry Blossom and sisters Hillside Lucetta and Hillside Valinda) in the Zawadzki pasture, I was led into their home called Middleholm, built in 1823. Here John, a dark-haired, soft-spoken chap with a professorial tone, has captured the true essence of the history of the breed with a museum-like collection of documents dating to the first years of their appearance in the Valley of the Clyde.

From John and Shona, an exuberant woman whose passion for Clydesdales is apparent, I learned much of the folklore and was able to inspect several publications dating back to the days when auctions drawing hundreds were held in Lanark where the heavy horses were bought and sold. Listening to this couple (Shona's heritage with the breed traces back to the 1800s) made me aware of the love they had for the Clydesdales, a true sentiment of everyone I have met who shares their lives with the breed.

While touring the countryside, John escorted me to the Strathaven Castle a few kilometers from Lesmahagow. It was once owned by the Dukes of Hamilton. Gazing at the ruins of the fifteenth century castle perched on a hillside made me realize the ancient ancestry of Clydesdales.

Tom Brewster, a bulky sort with a heavy Scottish brogue, whose grandfather first raised Clydesdales circa 1900, presented another view of the animal, one spirited by having grown up with them by his side. His photographic album traced many champions back to the nineteenth century. It provided another sense of the slice of history that comes with following the breed's evolution.

When I departed the Valley of the Clyde, it was with regret but also with more of a sense of the essence of the animal, one that first worked the fields helping farmers bring in their crops. Outside Lanark, as I drove toward Glasgow and Prestwick, I spied two in a pasture grazing without a care in the world. I quickly was transported into the mid-1800s and visualized a farmer stationed on a plow as two Clydesdales carried him across his land uncovering rich agricultural bounty.

To further educate myself about the breed, in 2004 I traveled on a wintry November day to Toronto, where The Royal Agricultural Winter Fair was being held. What an extravaganza, one featuring the finest of the heavy horses—Percherons, Belgians, and Clydesdales. Owners and breeders alike welcomed me as if I was a member of their family, and I learned much about a horse culture ripe with camaraderie and friendly competition.

In April, 2005, I attended the National Clydesdale Sale in Springfield, Illinois . What a spectacle this event is, with Clydesdale after Clydesdale being paraded into a huge show ring as enthusiastic horse lovers watch while the proud horses are auctioned. Being among the "Clydesdale family" once again was heartwarming since this group of owners and breeders enjoy a friendship that is most unique. How I enjoyed gathering additional insight into the history of the animal and collecting stories that caused me to laugh with the storyteller.

After watching the final sales of the Mares, I ventured to St. Louis where Budweiser official Jim Poole had arranged for me to tour Grant's Farm. Here Clydesdales roam the green grass and gawk at visitors. More than half a million people visit the compound every year free of charge, and being there is well worth it. Walking through Bauernhof Courtyard and looking at the Clydesdale memorabilia collected through the years provided a special bond with the Budweiser Clydesdales of old. Wandering through the stalls, I glimpsed Cindy, age four, and mother of the newest Clydesdale, Christina, just eighteen days old. I also met Billy Busch, a congenial man with a hearty handshake. He is the son of August A. Busch, Jr. whose passion for the breed helped save it from extinction in our country.

Near one of the pastures, I learned firsthand of the Clydesdale's friendly nature. As I walked up to one of the gates with my camera in hand, two sauntered over toward me as if to say, "Who are you, what are you doing here, and are you going to take our photograph?" As I edged closer to the fence, they walked right up to me and let me pet their soft faces. Then they posed together as I snapped several photographs. Once this was over, the two, apparently realizing the photo session was over, reversed course and headed toward their stalls where three or four other curious Clydes had watched us.

Despite my research and travels, no one can expect to cover every aspect of the Clydesdale story, even by visiting the land of their origin. My hope is that by presenting, among other things, a glimpse of their ancestors, a chronicle of their history, a composite of useful information about their characteristics, and stories about people who have bred and enjoyed the Clydesdales, this book will aid those that have the same questions about the Clydesdales I had when I began my journey to learn more about their mystical aura. I also trust that my writings will encourage those interested in owning one of these magical animals to do so, for there is not a more beautiful, more loveable, more loyal animal on the face of the earth.

— *Mark Shaw*

4 Kings
©C. Marcus Stone www.MarcusStone.com

"Yet, when all the books have been read and re-read, it boils down to the horse, his human companion, and what goes on between them."

—Walter Farley,
author of the
Black Stallion Series

The Magical Horse

Two Clydesdales enjoy the tranquility of a gentle pond owned by Bluffview Clydesdales,
Jack and Carol Angelbeck

The World's Most Magical Horse

A six-hitch Clydesdale team forges through the snow as the Budweiser jingle plays in the background

The familiar song, "Here comes the King, Here comes the big number One, Budweiser beer, the King, is Second to None," beats in the background as snow falls gently on a winding, winter trail.

The mountains in the background look like huge lumps of clay as several horses and a red and white four-wheeled wagon approach. The camera catches the freshness of the scene as the huge, wondrous animals, replete in their colorful harnesses, exhale a smattering of frost-covered breath. In unison, they trot toward the television screen as if to say "Hello, America, here's wishing you well."

These are the magical Clydesdales of Budweiser fame, the Hollywood version, stars in their own right. Like no animal before or since, they fill up the screen with their bulk, their sense of dignity and grace, as one foot, engulfed as it is in fluffy white feather, strides down the intended path. Even when there isn't the winter scene to accompany their sojourn, their proud stature overwhelms anything they surround.

The Clydesdale's entry into the entertainment arena follows that of many of its horse brethren. An image easy to recall is that of a bulky, white-winged horse stomping on the ground with great fury, causing water to spiral immediately from the earth. Thirsty, the mythical Pegasus gulped liquid from a spring that would become known as Hippocrene. Forever, those who would drink from "the fountain of inspiration" were blessed to write magical verses of poetry.

While Pegasus was certainly not a Clydesdale, he symbolizes the link between the arts and horses. In future generations, the breed would be featured in equestrian literature, art, sculpture, music, television, dance, theater, and film. By doing so, they would remind us that God's creatures, big and small, are indeed an extension of mankind, an integral part of the history of our very existence. Yet it is the horse, like few other animals, that is viewed with so many variables since it symbolizes strength and power, beauty and grace, speed and endurance, and a loyalty and obedience next to none.

Budweiser Clydesdales strut their high-stepping gait

The World's Most Magical Horse

The Mythical Pegasus
©Kinuko Y. Craft www.kycraft.com

As early as 1605, the horse was an integral part of literature when Spanish writer Miguel de Cervantes wrote *The Adventures of Don Quixote of La Mancha*, the tale of the irrepressible Don Quixote, his squire Sancho Panza, and a broken down horse, Rosinante. So named based on the words "rosin" (a drudge horse) and "ante" (before), this less than stellar animal (skin and bones) carried his rider to amorous adventures that have become legend.

In *Rockwood*, W. Harrison Ainsworth's classic 1834 novel, Black Bess carries his rider Dick Turpin almost 200 miles from London to York. The imagery is so vivid that many believe the tale to be true, even though it wasn't. Turpin, in fact, was an admirer of skullduggery, a "real person" who ended up being hung for murdering an innkeeper.

Black Beauty, published in 1877, is one of the most famous books featuring the horse as a main character. Not only was the story compelling, told from the carriage horse's perspective, but author Anna Sewell was able to use her words as social commentary to address the poor treatment of the breed in the mid-Victorian era.

The sport of polo served as a backdrop for Rudyard Kipling's 1895 novel, *The Maltese Cat*, a book chronicling the adventures of a waylaid, small, flea-bitten pony that is whisked from his home in Malta to India. Soon he is in the throes of the battle between the Skidars and the Archangels in Kipling's imaginative "Upper India Free-for-All Polo Cup." Given credit for the former's victory, he is dubbed, "Past Pluperfect Prestissimo Player of the Game."

In Enid Bagnold's 1935 novel, *National Velvet*, a horse named The Piebald captured the hearts of animal lovers and even those who cared little for the breed. Children were mesmerized by the tale of fourteen-year-old Velvet Brown, later to be played by Elizabeth Taylor in the film version. She wins the horse in a raffle and then sneaks her pride and joy into the Grand National steeplechase race. Velvet wins but is disqualified when she falls from the horse and is discovered to be a girl. No matter, by then readers' tears have been shed, and Velvet and her special horse are immortalized in the hearts and minds of those that treasure the story.

Black Beauty, the bestselling book

Art, with the horse as a main focus, has long been with us. Wall-drawings in the caves at Lascaux, France portray the amazing picture of a horse with black mane and brown markings as he gallops across the terrain. Some historians believe this art is more than 15,000 years old.

Amazing paintings were created by the nineteenth century artist Delacroix, whose love for Arabians is a staple in his works. His stallions have a certain fury about them and appear ready to leap off the canvas and race away towards the great outdoors. Another of Delacroix's ilk was Jacques-Louis David, a neo-classical artist who depicts Napoleon atop the mystical horse, Arab Marengo, in *Bonaparte Crossing the Saint-Bernard*.

The horse in sport has long been a favorite of artists such as Edgar Degas and George Stubbs. Whether it is man or woman with horse hunting, racing alone or with harness behind, or being shown in competition, the breed provides the perfect focus for portraying action that holds the viewer's eye.

The World's Most Magical Horse

Armageddon's Stallion
©C. Marcus Stone www.MarcusStone.com

Horses at war have also provided a backdrop for featuring the horse in art. None had more talent than Frederic Remington, known as "the artist of the West." His Civil War masterpiece, *Into Battle*, is a classic depicting riders with guns at the ready atop horses scampering at full speed toward the enemy. A close look shows that the faces of the animals indicate a determination parallel to that of the soldiers as their bodies dip toward the ground at full speed. Remington was also responsible for *Dash For The Timber* and the treasured sculpture *The Magnificent Man*.

Modern day artists who have captured the magic of the Clydesdale include Persis Clayton Weirs and Chris Cummings of Hill City, South Dakota. The latter's *Snow Kings* is a classic. Another is C. Marcus Stone. Her paintings include *Among Friends, Ready For Show, Black Oak Clydes,* and *Armageddon's Stallion*.

Sculptors have long loved the horse, molding statues that are pleasing to the eye and provide a reference for their incredible hulk and ability to carry soldiers and the common man alike. In Venice, a grand horse stands with left foot raised carrying a sturdy mount with steadfast face. It was created by Renaissance sculptor Andrea del Verrochio more than five hundred years ago.

Television has never shied away from using the horse as a central character in its programming or, as in the case of the Budweiser Clydesdales, commercials. One of the most famous horses in history is Trigger, Roy Rogers's gold and white Palomino. The do-gooder "King of the Cowboys," with wife Dale Evans alongside, catapulted the horse into prominence as a loyal friend to be counted on even when a dastardly band of outlaws threatened to shoot Roy through the eyes. A natural in front of the camera, Trigger mesmerized those that knew him since he was the ultimate trick horse whose repertoire included dance steps, yawning, dipping, whinnying on cue, and believe it or not, the ability to walk backwards more than 150 paces. Trigger lived to be thirty-three years old, equivalent to a human living past the century mark. Other famous "wild west film horse stars" include Wild Bill Hickock's Buckshot, Dale Evans's Buttermilk, Gene Autry's Champion, The Cisco Kid's Diablo, The Lone Ranger's Silver, and Topper William Boyd, Hopalong Cassidy's sidekick.

> *How many Clydesdales are born each year?*
>
> The United States has the largest number of Clydesdales, with Canada, Great Britain, and Australia trailing. There are over 600 new Clydesdales registered in the United States annually.

As early as the days when fans watched movies without sound, the horse was a star. William S. Hart's sidekick, Fritz the Pinto, made an appearance in the film, one where neither of the main characters used any doubles. This was also true of Tony The Wonder Horse, Tom Mix's partner in such films as *Hard Boiled*. He was quite the trickster, rescuing his friend from precarious situations by untying rope, becoming a messenger who sought help, and actually fighting alongside terrible Tom using his hoofs and teeth. Tony became so famous that he starred in his own film, *Just Tony*, before dying at age 34.

Early on, when the Clydesdales were being established by the Anheuser-Busch brewery as a symbol of excellence, a short film called *Big Scot, The Story of a Champion* was produced. It proved to be quite popular and provided audiences with more information about the mystical horse.

While a horse's head positioned in a bed is used to scare the bejesus out of an arrogant Hollywood film director in *The Godfather*, many forget that the species was also employed by director Francis Ford Coppola in the theater scene in Sicily where actor Al Pacino's son performs in the opera. Horses also play an integral role in such films as *Gladiator* where they pull chariots in the Coliseum, *The Horse Whisperer* with Robert Redford, and *Seabiscuit*, the improbable book-to-film story of a smallish thoroughbred that outlasts the seemingly unbeatable War Admiral in a match race to win the hearts of a country knee-deep in tough financial times.

Heavy horses are featured in many films, including producer/actor Mel Gibson's classic, *Braveheart*. It featured the folk hero William Wallace, whose statue graces

Roy Rogers and Trigger, his famous sidekick

St. Nicholas Parish in Lanark in the Valley of the Clyde.

Adding to the folklore of Clydesdales is their appearance in three films: a "walk-on" in *Hello Dolly*; a part in the Jerry Lewis film, *Hardly Working*; and prominence in *Country Fair*, starring Henry Fonda. In each film, audiences cheer the Clydesdales as they appear on the big screen.

Whether the Clydesdales are looked upon as symbols of power and grandeur or are simply pets to be cared for in a quiet pasture, these animals are as much a part of life as any of the horses, real or mythical, that ever lived. There is a true romance with the animal for it epitomizes all that is revered about horses in general. Not a day goes by when there isn't an "ooh" or an "aah" when someone spies this mystical animal with the tradition of a high-stepping gait.

Majestic in appearance, mystical in folklore, loyal, calm, all that and more, is the Clydesdale. With a peek into how their horse brethren first appeared on the horizon, it is possible to trace their origin from before the days of Christ to a waterfall in Scotland called Clyde.

The statue of folk hero William Wallace, made famous in the film Braveheart

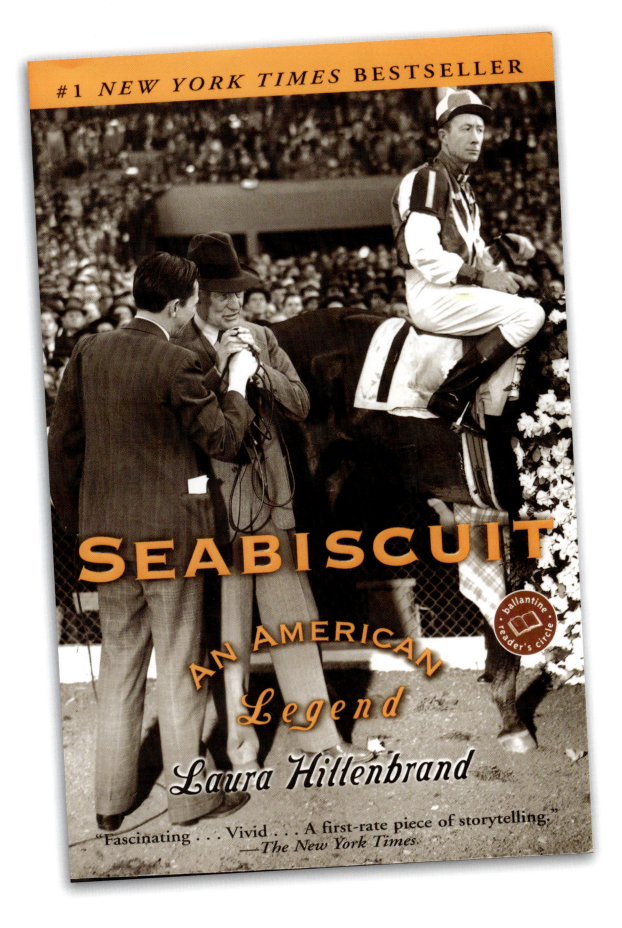

Seabiscuit, the little horse that could

"A lovely horse is always an experience . . . It is an emotional experience of the kind that is spoiled by words."

— Beryl Markham,
West With The Night

The Horse, Of Course

Two curious Clydesdales in the Scottish countryside

*Without the horse,
wars would have been lost.*

*Without the horse,
food would have been scarce.*

*Without the horse,
transportation would
have been impossible.*

*Without the horse,
forests never would
have been cleared.*

*Without the horse,
people in olden days would
have had no carriages to ride.*

Charles Pritchard competes at the 2004 Columbus Carriage Days

Ah yes, the horse, of course – a most important beast since no other animal subservient to men has influenced mankind's survival like the wondrous horse and, particularly, the heavy horse.

What is a "heavy horse?" This question is answered only if one researches the history of horses to gain an understanding of where they came from, how they evolved, how they came into favor, and why for centuries they, with all due respect to the dog, are truly man's best friend. This fact is bolstered when one considers the inability of dogs to plow, to be ridden with a saddle, or to draw the weight of a Budweiser hitch wagon.

Horses in general were believed to have originated from God's hand according to the word of Genesis (man's origins can only be traced some 50,000 years ago—horses between 50 and 100 *million* years ago).

While many swear this is so, renowned British naturalist Charles Darwin believed, as stated in his 1859 book *On the Origin of Species by Means of Natural Selection*, that all such creatures evolved according to something he called "Natural Selection, a process akin not so much to the survival of the fittest but the development and change of an individual species over succeeding generations," as explained in *The New Rider's Horse Encyclopedia*.

Regardless, much research has been conducted into the origin of the horse using cave paintings, fossils, and rock formations. This indicates that early ancestors of the horse roamed the earth millions of years ago. Of them, most prominent was "The Dawn Horse," a round-backed animal with four toes on the front feet and three on the back. It was small in stature, no bigger than a good-sized black Labrador or a large cat, standing less than fourteen inches tall and weighing somewhere in the neighborhood of twelve pounds.

The Dawn Horse stood only 14 inches high

Merychippus: a faster horse that its predecessors

Evolution

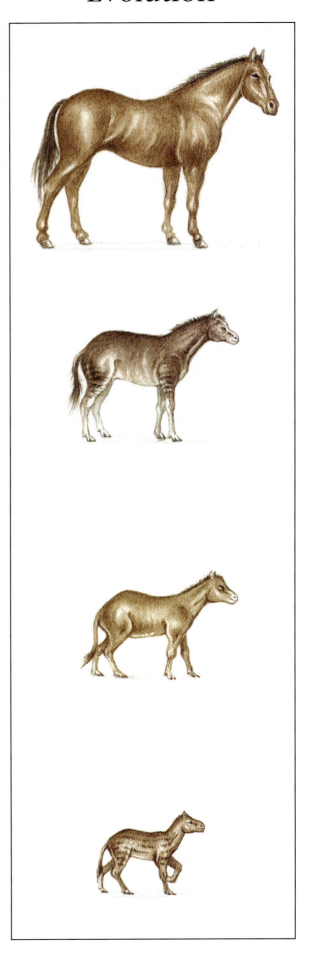

This horse was dubbed an "Eohippus." Its characteristics included padded feet that enabled it to traverse wet surfaces such as were located in jungles. A spotted coat permitted nondisclosure, with the skin rough like that of a deer. Conjecture is that the animal possessed eyes that were centrally located on the head, not on the sides as with future species. Teeth were short-crowned, preventing the chewing of anything more than leaves and brush.

When skeletons were discovered, first in Wyoming in the 1860s, and then in the same state some seventy years later, the above-mentioned characteristics were confirmed. But scientists believe that this breed of horse became extinct more than 40 million years ago, with the progression toward Equus caballus, the tagline for the modern horse, to follow.

This it did, and the Eohippus was replaced by the Mesohippus and Miohippus. These horses were more advanced, especially in the mouth area where incisor teeth permitted them to chomp on more tasty delights. Improvement in the feet included three toes on each foot, and longer legs were prevalent. This apparently permitted the horse to not only defend its existence by concealment but scamper across the wilderness to escape a foe.

Twenty to twenty-five million years ago, the above breeds were replaced by the Merychippus. Scientists continued to believe that the evolution of this species was dictated by its environment in that much of the jungle was now "steppelands," treeless terrain that permitted no concealment. To avoid extinction, the Merychippus had longer legs to permit a faster pace with the weight of the horse, increasing as time passed, carried on the center toe.

To permit more vision, this breed possessed a longer neck. When it raised its head, it could see further. Eyes were now on the side of the head, and teeth were stronger and higher-crowned with enamel facing allowing the horse's menu to increase through the years.

Pliohippus: The first single-hoofed horse

Next up was the Pliohippus, arriving according to the above-mentioned encyclopedia, during the mid-Pleistocene period some six million years ago. It featured the first single-hoofed horse, one complete with fully developed leg ligaments. Heights soared to more than 50 inches, or 12 hands or so in horse language. It is suspected that this species was responsible for the modern day ass (hemionids or half-asses) and zebras.

To bring the horse into prominence, along came the Equus caballas, dubbed "the true forerunner of the modern horse." It originated five million years later during the second half of the Ice Age.

This breed, believed to have roamed South America, Asia, Europe, and even Africa, was spotted in 9000 BC. Since the last land bridge across the Bering Strait had been severed, horses disappeared from the North American landscape, not to return until sixteen of the beauties were re-introduced by the Spanish explorer Hernando Cortes during the early sixteenth century.

While North America was horseless, other continents were not. Western Asia and Europe possessed the horse, while the zebras and asses traversed to North and South Africa. Modern horses have been traced to the Asiatic Wild Horse (also known as "Przewalski's Horse," so named because it was located on Mongolia's Gobi Desert by Russian Colonel Nikolai Przewalski in 1879), the Tarpan (means "wild horse," S. S. Gmelin found them in 1768), and the Forest Horse. The latter is important, for the heavy horse is said to have originated with this species.

For years, horse experts swear that big horses descend from one of two primitive types: the "northern cold-blooded type" or the "southern warm-blooded." Of the two, the former, the northern (Equus caballus frigidus for Latin lovers) was the most important contributor to the modern heavy horse.

Horse historians surmise that this breed roamed the plains of Europe and Asia in prehistoric centuries since they are depicted in cave drawings. Apparently man's relationship with them was simple; they were used for hunting, and they were hunted, as in "I'm looking for a tasty dinner." The former appears true since during the Late Bronze Age, graves were discovered in Britain containing bits and bridles. Regarding the latter, horsemeat was looked upon as quite edible, even without the modern condiments.

While the British breeds are suspected of being small in stature, Roman times produced larger animals, thought to be a product of, according to the book *Gentle Giants*

What is a Clydesdale?

Clydesdales are a breed of heavy draft horse. Clydesdales originated from Scottish farm horses over two hundred years ago.

The World's Most Magical Horse

Drum Horse: Blue Roan Clydesdale and rider of the Household Cavalry, in full parade costume.
The rider's uniform is embroidered with gold thread and the silver drums weigh 68 kg each

by Ralph Whitlock, "Fairly massive, heavy-headed animals with bristly manes which had been domesticated by German tribes living on the plains and in the forests of central Europe." Folklore has it that the Greeks, when they spied a horse and rider on the horizon, believed that it was simply one and the same. Julius Caesar noted that the Gallic Army used "heavy horses to transport supplies" and, believing they could be used by his soldiers in combat, ordered several to be shipped to Rome for cross-breeding.

As with modern romance, the "northern breed" and the "southern breed" apparently became smitten with one another and were crossbred. This occurred between 2000 and 1000 BC. For reasons unknown, the southern breed was dominant, and thus the Arabic horses possessed both speed and beauty—like blue bloods of a sort.

Taking horses into battle apparently occurred when leaders of the day realized that fighting hand-to-hand combat made little sense. Folklore spins the tale that the legendary King Arthur was one of the first to enlist large beasts to carry his soldiers into the fray. As armor became more and more laborious, the horse (poor thing) was saddled with the responsibility of carrying not only the knight, but also his full weight of enclosure (perhaps weighing three hundred pounds or more). As stated in *Gentle Giants*, "The Great Horse of Europe was thus evolved as a war horse, a corollary of the knight in armor."

Evidence exists in Western European paintings and tapestries, mostly in battle scenes, and proclamations that Kings and chieftains rode what were dubbed "high horses" to note their importance. Besides King Arthur and his famous Round Table, others of note linked with the heavy horses were Ivanhoe, Sir Lancelot, and Sir Galahad. All learned that the forward thrust of the horse permitted them to fling their spears with greater acceleration and, most times, accuracy.

This "beat 'em up with strength" concept worked well until many of the armies floundered when fighting foes in the West equipped with the Arabic specimens that were fleet afoot. The heavier horses stalled as the quicker breeds flitted about, providing a distinct advantage.

From the sixteenth century, horses gradually began replacing oxen in art and plough. These were strong beasts, as evidenced by a passage in *Gentle Giants* where the author writes, "In Tudor times it has been stated that five or six cart horses would draw a burden of 3,000 lb. weight 'for a long journey.' Even some of the pack horses must have been strong, upstanding animals, for they could carry burdens of up to four hundred-weights without strain." This belief would carry over into the early 1900s based on a statement in *The Clydesdales International Magazine* attributed to Archibald MacNeilage, editor of The *Scottish Farmer*. He said, "A draught horse must be capable of drawing, and the best type for that purpose is the Clydesdale, sound in feet and limb, with deep well-ribbed barrel, powerfully developed forearms and thighs, long quarters and short back, intelligent head and good, straight action, more pleasing in its perfection when walking than when giving a showy display of the trot."

By the seventeenth century, heavy horses had been immersed not only into agriculture, but into daily life as well. This occurred through their use in pulling coaches, although some of the horses were smaller in stature than those used on the farms. Nevertheless, they were strong animals able to pull the cart at good speed with passengers and a driver.

Another novel use of the heavy horse (draft or draught, the British spelling, originates from the old English word meaning "pulling"—draft beer is drawn or pulled from kegs) occurred when canals became popular

Chistopher Hone drives the Diamond Z Ranch hitch team of English Shires in the Ketchum (Idaho) Wagon Days Parade during the 2002 Labor Day weekend

'Hold, Sir Dragon!' shouted Sir Lancelot

The immortal Sir Lancelot fighting Dragon on horseback

and barges became favorable. The curious decided that horses with some stature could pull the barge while walking along the shore. Soon this was commonplace, mostly carried out by lighter crossbreds.

To understand the development of the magnificent Clydesdales, it is important to know a bit about the English Shire, so named from the counties of Staffordshire, Derbyshire, and Leicestershire. Along with Fen Country, these were the principal breeding areas.

The Shire, in turn, was a by-product of the Flanders Horse, imported into England during the seventeenth century. Characteristics include four colors: grey, brown, black, and bay; the height: a minimum of 16 hands to 19, averaging somewhere in the 17s; the head: masculine, long, and thin; a long neck in proportion; eyes well set; feet: wide and solid; and hair: thinnish, straight, and silky. Weight varied between 1800 and 2200 pounds.

The Shire was a workhorse, a cart horse. At one time, more than 90% of the cart horses in England were Shires. A celebrated

The Clydesdales as workhorses plowing a field

Shire stallion was the legendary Blind Horse of Packington. He appeared in the mid-1700s. In 1880, Shires were showed and the king of the lot was Admiral 71, the champion at the annual Spring Show in the Royal Agricultural Winter Fair Hall at Islington. He was so touted that a breeder in Australia purchased him for export to the tune of nearly fifteen hundred pounds, a huge amount in those days.

A Chicago Union Stock Yard Clydesdale Four Horse Hitch at Stock Yard Inn.
The hotel catered exclusively to live stock producers and farmers

The World's Most Magical Horse

Back view of Clydesdales plowing a field

The Shire was not a speed horse, but it was strong, had stamina, and was adaptable. So docile is the animal that there is folklore to the effect that when it stops to rest it actually falls asleep.

Speaking of strength, a Shire Horse Society publication related that two such animals once pulled nearly *nineteen tons*. On another occasion, the Shires pulled a dynamometer (a device used to measure power) that weighed almost fifty tons.

If the Shire made England proud, it was the Clydesdale that put Scotland on the horse map. As was the case with other familiar animal types and strains that originated in this land, such as Angus, Scotch Shorthorn, Collie, Shetland, and Blackface, the Clydesdale's appearance would rival that of Scotch whiskey in the recognition arena.

Debate continues to this day as to the actual origin of the breed since two feuding groups, the Clydesdale Horse Society of Great Britain and Ireland and the Select Clydesdale Society of Scotland (it lasted only a few years), present conflicting viewpoints. There is conjecture that one of the Dukes of Hamilton (the Sixth seems the best guess) imported several black Flemish stallions (one of them dark brown in color) into Scotland in the mid-1700s for use of the tenants and crossed them with native Scots mares on their estates around Strathaven and Lesmahagow in the mid-seventeenth century.

Owned by the Dukes at that time was Strathaven Castle, also known as Avondale Castle, situated, according to a plaque nearby, "on a rocky outcrop on the banks of the Pow-millon Burn." Built around 1458, it fell into ruin in the eighteenth century, but in its prime was unique as a "Tower House built on the plan of a parallelogram, with two towers at diagonally opposite corners, five stories high with walls ten foot thick, crowned with a battlement some five feet higher than the roof." In 1611, after several changes of "ownership," the castle was sold to James II, Marquis of Hamilton. He and his clan owned it for the next three hundred years with folklore alleging that when the wife of a Lord so displeased her husband she was walled up alive in part of the castle wall. When part of the wall fell down during the nineteenth century, bones were discovered providing credibility to the story.

Tony Bowers of Sparta, Wisconsin drives through the woods on the Don Hahn Farm near Cashton with a Shire pair named Walker and Domino of Brightenridge Farm leading the way

The Geat American Clydesdale

A team of Clydesdales thunder through a plowed field

STRATHAVEN CASTLE

Situated on a rocky outcrop on the banks of the Powmillon Burn, Strathaven Castle (also known as Avondale Castle) has a long and turbulent history. The present Castle was built around 1458, on the site of earlier structures. Since then it has undergone many changes. The Castle has associations with the Hamilton family and the Covenanters. It finally fell into ruin in the 18th Century.

Historical Background

The first stone castle on the site was erected in the 14th Century, probably replacing an earlier wooden structure. This castle was built by either the Baird or Fleming families, both of whom owned large areas of land in Avondale at that time.

By the 1400's, the Castle and lands belonged to the notorious Douglas family. In 1450, Strathaven became a Royal Burgh, as a reward for the Douglases giving support and military aid to King James II. Soon, however, the family became too powerful and rebelled against the Crown, resulting in the suppression of the House of Douglas in 1455. According to Gray's *Chronicles*, "in the month of March 1455, Strathaven Castle was burned down and the possessions of the Douglases were confiscated and given up to fire and sword".

A new castle was built on the site around 1458 by Sir Andrew Stewart, who became the 1st Lord Avondale. The Castle remained in the hands of the Stewart family until 1534, when a feud with neighbours brought change. The 3rd Lord was forced to exchange the Castle and Barony of Avondale with Sir James Hamilton of Finnart (a famous architect of his day), for the Barony of Ochiltree in Ayrshire. During Sir James's occupation, the Castle was strengthened and enlarged.

Crest of the Barony of Avondale.

The legend of Strathaven Castle on a plaque outside

Why the Dukes became enamored with a new breed of animals that would be known as Clydesdale is unclear, but no doubt their agricultural needs necessitated the requirement for such a breed. One can only imagine them deciding that combining the beauty of the Flemish stallions with the bulk of native Scottish mares made perfect sense.

This scenario conflicts with what appears to be irrefutable evidence that the breed first appeared in the eighteenth century (around 1752) when they were spotted in the lowlands around Lanarkshire, near the Falls of Clyde, located south of Glasgow. Given credit for the majestic horse was a tenant farmer named John Paterson from Lochlyoch, Carmichael. According to the author of *Gentle Giants*, he "imported a black stallion from Flanders, which had considerable influence on the breed." This occurred nearly four hundred years after William, Earl of Douglas obtained a permit from King Edward III of England to bring ten big Flemish horses to the valley circa 1352.

This development coincided with the need for heavy horses to assist with agricultural requirements in addition to providing transportation. Regarding the former, the Clydesdale would have been especially effective in muddy terrain or on the steep hills where it was difficult to maneuver or climb.

To promote the notion, the Highland and Agricultural Society of Scotland was organized in 1784. In 1826, they held a grand show with awards being promised for those Clydesdales from Lanark, Renfrew, Dumbarton, Stirling, and Ayr. In 1870, the annual Glasgow Stallion Show was held, featuring the finest stallions of the era.

Strathaven Castle where the Duke of Hamilton resided

Veteran Clydesdale Stallions at Glasgow Stallion Show, 1938

Seven years later, the renowned Clydesdale Horse Society was organized. Its first historical publication listed more than 1000 stallions and nearly 500 mares. Standards for the breed were stated in the *Standard Cyclopedia of Modern Agriculture*. They included:

"The Clydesdale is a very active horse. He is not bred for action, like the Hackney, but he must have action . . . The foot at every step must be lifted clean off the ground, and the inside of every shoe be made plain to the man standing behind . . . The forelegs must be planted well under the shoulders - not on the outside, like the legs of a bulldog - and the legs must be plumb and, so to speak, hang straight from the shoulder to the fetlock joint. There must be no openness at the knees, and no inclination to knock the knees together. In like manner, the hind legs must be planted closely together with the points of the hocks turned inwards rather than outwards; the thighs must well down to the hocks, and the shanks from the hock joint to the fetlock must be plumb and straight. 'Sickle' hocks are a very bad fault, as they lead to loss of leverage.

The famous Falls of Clyde gush down the countryside near Lanarkshire, Scotland

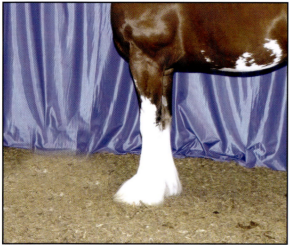

The feather on Grandview Eli's Intrigue

the mid-section of Grandview Eli's Intrigue

[The feet] must be open and round, like a mason's mallet. The hoof heads must be wide and springy, with no suspicion of hardness such as may lead to the formation of a sidebone or ringbone . . . A Clydesdale should have a nice open forehead, broad between the eyes; a flat (neither Roman-nosed or "dished") profile; a wide muzzle; large nostrils; a bright, clear, intelligent eye; a big ear, and a well-arched, long neck springing out of an oblique shoulder, with high withers.

[The Clydesdale's] back should be short, and ribs well-sprung from the backbone, like the hoops of a barrel. His quarters should be long, and his thighs well packed with muscle and sinew. He should have broad, clean, sharply developed hocks, and big knees, broad in front. The impression created by a thoroughly well-built Clydesdale is that of strength and activity, with minimum of superfluous tissue. The idea is not grossness and bulk, but quality and weight.

the facial features of Grandview Eli's Intrigue

Grandview Eli's Intrigue

The ideal colour for a Clydesdale is dark brown, with a more or less defined white stripe on his face, dark-coloured fore-legs, and white hind shanks."

These guidelines are as relevant today as they were nearly two hundred years ago. A basic difference would be that the colors of the modern Clydesdale lean more to bays, browns, and blacks with four white legs. Whatever the preference, the magnificence continues since the Clydesdale is a breed like no other in the world.

The Magical Clydesdale

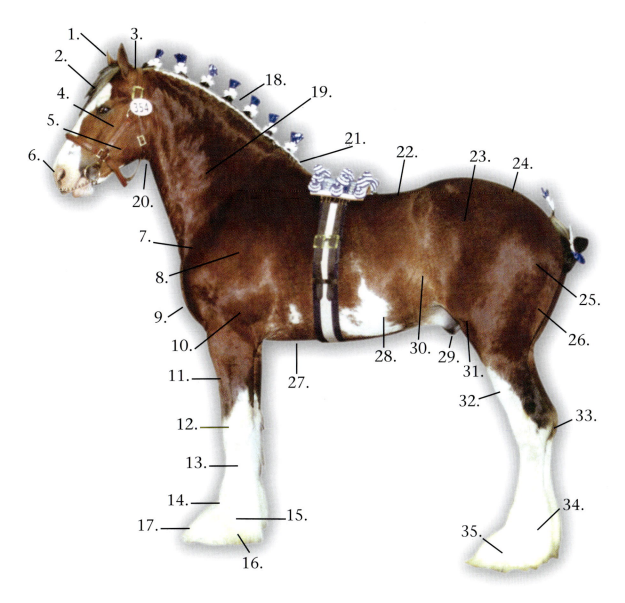

SBH Phoenix and all of his parts
SBH Phoenix is owned by Wismer Clydesdales

1. Ear
2. Forelock
3. Poll
4. Cheekbone
5. Cheek
6. Nose
7. Slope of shoulder
8. Shoulder bed
9. Breast
10. Arm
11. Forearm
12. Knee
13. Cannon
14. Fetlock
15. Pastern
16. Heel
17. Hoof
18. Mane
19. Neck
20. Throatlatch
21. Withers
22. Back
23. Hip
24. Croup
25. Quarters
26. Thigh
27. Underline
28. Barrel
29. Sheath
30. Flank
31. Stifle
32. Gaskin
33. Hock
34. Feather
35. Foot

"Sell the cow, buy the sheep, but never be without the horse."

—Irish Proverb

The Magnificent Clydesdales

A Scottish Clydesdale

Those inquisitive about Clydesdales ask primarily the same questions today as they did a hundred years ago:

How tall are Clydesdales?
They may grow to 19 hands tall. In human terms that is about six feet four inches (one hand equals four inches). They are measured from the ground to the withers. It is located at the end of the horse's mane. When the horse puts its head down to eat, this is the highest point on the horse.

How much do Clydesdales weigh?
From 1600 to 2400 pounds, or nearly as much as a Volkswagen Beetle.

What are possible Clydesdale colors?
Mostly bay or brown, but they can be black or sorrel. They can be roan. This is any color with white hair scattered throughout the coat (occasionally seen). A white blaze face and four white legs are common, but black legs do appear.

Why do Clydesdales have so much hair on their legs?
This long, flowing hair is called feather or spat. It originally protected the hooves, but is now mostly for show.

How large are Clydesdales' hooves?
A typical horseshoe is about the size of a dinner plate. They are held in place with nails that are pounded into the hoof wall, an act that does not hurt the horse.

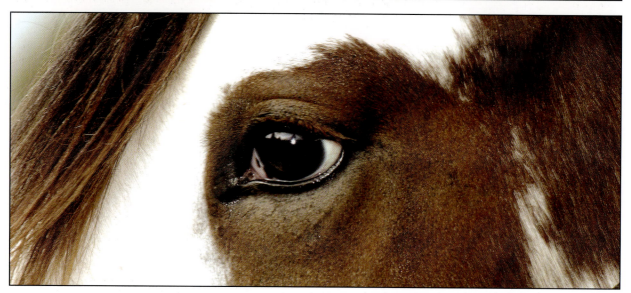

Eye of Clydesdale, owned by Jim and Judy Holt

Some people are curious about how much a Clydesdale eats. Depending on age, an adult will consume 25 to 50 pounds of hay and 2 to 10 pounds of grain each day.

If one examines all these characteristics closely, it is easy to see the similarities between the Clydesdale and the English Shire. This said, proud Clydesdale owners like to boast that their breed is more active, enjoys a bit more speed, and has more of a personality. To them, there is only one horse to own and that is the Clydesdale.

When discussing the "senses" of the Clydesdale, fact must be separated from fiction. Their ability to smell is extraordinary, taste apparently excellent, touch average or better. They are able to hear from great distances since, like humans, they have binaural

2S Maxton Prince Charles, owned by Jim and Judy Holt of Cypress Creek Clydesdales, Cypress Texas, bred by Pat McMahen of 2S Clydesdales

Clydesdales owned by Jim and Judy Holt grazing in the pasture

hearing, meaning they can hear from both ears at the same time. Unlike humans, Clydesdales can move and swivel their ears around like antennae to pick up sounds.

The Clydesdales' sight is enhanced since their large eyes are positioned to the sides of their head instead of in front like many animals. Some say they can see more than 340 degrees and this appears possible. Their only blind spots may be straight ahead and directly behind.

Those that believe Clydesdales can actually see everything in double size appear to be stretching the truth a bit. But veterinarian Dr. Martin English says, in general, that "horses can see some color—yellow, green, and blue with color diminishing with decreasing light."

Clydesdales enjoy food that tastes sweet or salty. This keeps them from eating plants that may be poisonous since most of them have a bitter taste, including buttercups, the yellow-flowered weed containing juices that may injure a horse's digestive system and blister their skin. Another dreaded enemy (when left on the ground) is the leaf of the Red Maple.

Clydesdales are friendly with most animals, including donkeys, dogs, and goats. Some like pigs, some don't. Perhaps it's their high-pitched squeal. Opossums are a threat to horses of any kind, especially the pink-nosed, black-eyed, rat-tailed ones, because they can carry a parasite that causes a debilitating disease in horses.

The origin of the Clydesdale, as stated, is traced to the area in and around Lanarkshire, formerly known as Clydesdale. It is located in southeast Scotland, where bagpipes instill a mood of serenity and tradition. This is a fertile valley where Flemish and Dutch stallions were stationed to service the mares of the area, with the idea to increase the size and strength of the breed. The draft horse resulted, ones such as Blaze, a black stallion born in 1779. His characteristics included a wide, white stripe in the middle of his face, and four pure-white, knee-length stockings. Blaze and his brethren were named after the valley from which they originated, a tribute to the River Clyde and the district of Clydesdale.

Lets snuggle up together

This folklore was memorialized in *The Clydesdales Breed, The Finest Draught Horses In The World*, a publication released by the Clydesdales Horse Society of Great Britain and Ireland in 1938. It begins with the words, "The modern history of the breed begins about the middle of the eighteenth century, when the native hardy breed found in Lanarkshire, through which the River Clyde flows, was being graded up to greater weight and substance by the use of Flemish stallions, and at least one outstanding native stallion named Blaze which was brought from Ayrshire into the Upper Ward of Lanarkshire. Clydesdale is the old name for Lanarkshire, just as the Mearns is the old name for Kincardinshire, Angus for Forfarshire, Tweeddale for Peeblesshire, and the Merse for Berwickshire."

Regarding the use for the new heavy breed, the publication pronounces, "The Clydesdale breed is the breed whose characteristics and type for purposes of draught were moulded by the farmers of the Upper Ward of Lanarkshire to meet the demands of commerce when the coalfields of Lanarkshire began to be developed, roads to be improved, and haulage by the shoulder to be substituted for carriage on the back of the native breed of horses."

The publication reports that, ironically, one of the first of the breed to be baptized with honor was a horse named Clyde, who won first prize at the Glasgow Cattle Market in 1844. This was some eighteen years after classes for agriculture horses were permitted at the Highland and Agricultural Society's shows.

Historians point to many famous Clydesdales, triggering interest in the breed. Among them is Glancer, also known as Thompson's Black Horse, owned by James Thompson of Germiston, Tolleross, Glasgow. Lampit's Farm's Mr. Somerville was the breeder. He became the great-grand-sire of Broomfield Champion. He arrived somewhere around 1830 and the lineage of many of the great champions such as Clyde, Farmer's Fancy, Salmond's Champion, and Darnley are traced to him.

The famous Prince of Wales

Clydesdales with significant contribution to the modern era are Prince of Wales 673 and Darnley 222. The Prince boasted "heavy bone and good mature weight of 2,200 pounds [with] good feet and legs and moved with the best of them," according to *Heavy Horses* by Grant MacEwan. He boasted of Hiawatha, a horse bred in 1892, and one whose show ring prowess was next to none, including four times winning the Cawdor Cup, first donated by the Earl of Cawdor, the top prize in the breed. Hiawatha lived to the ripe old age of twenty-three.

Darnley 222 was as impressive as Prince of Wales, weighing nearly the same with outstanding features. In a stirring article written for the Spring 2004 *Draft Horse Journal*, historian Jim Emmons chronicles the evolution of Darnley 222, described as being a "dark dappled bay color with a white right hind leg up midway to the hock." Symbolizing the astonishing links to modern day Clydesdales, Emmons begins his tale nearly 125 years ago with the mating of the mare Keir Peggy with the three-year-old Conqueror 199 in Dunblane, Scotland. Keir Peggy's owner was Sir William Stirling Maxwell. Five years later, Darnley 222 captured first prize at the Glasgow Stallion Show, the premier event of its time. Sons included Top Gallant, MacGregor, Lord Blantyre, Sanquhar, and Flashwood. McQueen, son of MacGregor, traversed the Atlantic to Madison, Wisconsin when Robert B. Ogilivie purchased him in the mid-1880s. Top Gallant, according to Emmons, then sired Sir Everard 5353 in 1885, and he in turn produced a son, Baron's Pride 9122, called "possibly the greatest breeding horse of all time" by the historian. His son, a two-year-old named Benedict, was then exported to the United States in 1898 to Brookside Farms in Fort Wayne, Indiana.

Baron's Pride

Remarkably, Baron's Pride, as Emmons points out, "sired eight champions (six sons and two mares) at the Chicago International from 1900-1913." Eleven Cawdor Cup champions would also be sired by the miracle horse with every winner after 1905 being traced to him. No wonder Emmons makes the bold statement, "It is safe to say that every Clydesdale on the face of the earth is a descendant of Baron's Pride."

Another horse of note was Broomfield Champion, also known as Aberdeen Champion. His son was Clyde alias Glancer, who had seven sons that traveled to districts such as Renfrewshire, Ayrshire, Midlothian, Bute, Wigtownshire, and Kintyre. Around 1840, as reported by The Clydesdale Breed, "this movement of the breed, and of the Muir family from Sornfallo on the slopes of Tinto in Lanarkshire to farms in Galloway, a notable transference of Clydesdales of the most approved type took place, and results

Darnley 222

can be traced to this day through the influence of a sire like, say Lochfergus Champion. Agnew's Farmer, which won first at the H. & A. S. Show at Dumfries in 1830, was got by a horse called Clydeside, whose name bespeaks his origin."

In modern Lanarkshire, where the Clydesdales were used for both town and farm work, those who live near the Falls of Clyde still savor the animal and their memories of old. Reminders of the horse are everywhere from the Clydesdale banks to the Clydesdale Inn in Lanark.

Love for the Clydesdales burns bright as evidenced by the words of John Zawadzki, publisher of *The Clydesdales International Magazine*. Owner, along with wife Shona, of 2000 Cawdor Cup champion Hillside Lorton Legend, they continue to be fascinated with this ancient animal. "Clydesdales are a touch with the past," John says, "a rare breed, a gentle animal like no other." Shona adds,

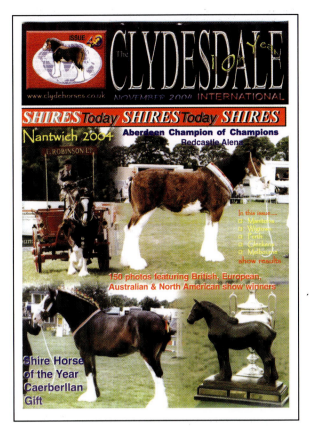

The Clydesdale International Magazine, spreading news about Clydesdales through out the world

Scottish Clydesdale historian John Zawadzki and wife Shona

"Once you get the Clydesdale bug, you are hooked and you get sort of a disease, a wonderful disease at that."

For Canadian Ronnie Wismer, the love of the animal is because "they are the smartest of the draft horses and thus easier to train, not high strung, not banging on bars like other breeds." New York breeder Mary Flinn says, "I like all that hair, until, of course, I have to wash it."

To Greenwood Farms breeder Charles Cryderman, his affinity for the wondrous horse is simple. "Nothing in the world is prettier than a Clydesdale," he swears.

Jack Shaw, owner with wife Sue of Great American Clydesdales, has a pat answer for those who wonder why he is fascinated with Clydesdales. "I tell them," he says, "that it may sound corny, but I think Clydesdales stand for everything that is good about the U.S.A. and the world. They have strength, yet are gentle. And they have pride and dignity and a sense of humor."

Clydesdale Bank in Lanarkshiree, Scotland

Perhaps it is Richard Wegner, the noted Clydesdale expert, who summarizes the love for the breed. At his farm in Clinton, Michigan, two good-sized humps are visible above ground beside an apple tree in his yard. There lies the mare Meadowview Oracle, and the stallion, Solomon's Commodore, two of Richard's prized Clydesdales. The latter was purchased when Richard was just a budding breeder.

"When I first saw him," Wegner recalls, "I peeked into his stall. Then I began talking to him, calling him Buddy since I didn't know his real name. When he seemed friendly, I entered the stall and patted him a bit. Later, I returned with three or four breeders whose opinions I trusted. I said, 'Do you see anything wrong with him?' When they said 'no,' I bought the horse. He turned out to be a real winner, breeding such horses as Maplewood Commodore's John, later shown as Joker. He won everything, some calling him the perfect Clydesdale. When Commodore died, I thought it was fitting that he lay resting in the yard along with Meadowview Oracle since they were part of the family for so long."

To Wegner, like other Clydesdale owners, there is a certain something about the breed that separates them from their heavy horse brethren, something that is mysterious, mystical. "With all due respect to the Belgians, the Percherons, and the others," he says, "there is a different aura about the Clydesdales, a little more flair. That is what I love about them."

Richard Wegner and Solomon's Commodore, buried in Wegner's yard

Stanley White drives the Unicorn for White Rock Clydesdales Argyle, Texas
at the 2004 National Show

"I love the horse from hoof to head.
From head to hoof and tail to mane.
I love the horse as I have said?
From head to hoof and back again."

James Whitcomb Riley,
— *I Love The Horse*

The International Clydesdales

If Baron's Pride was not the greatest breeding Clydesdale of all time
his grandson, Dunure Footprint, was

Grey Percheron Stallion, Blizzard won Grand Champion at many shows. Bred by Bob and Marilyn Robinson of Richland, Michigan

The Shire, the Percheron, the Belgian Heavy Draught, the Ardennes, the Australian Draught, the Boulonnais, the Breton, the Dutch Heavy Draught, the Hungarian Heavy Draught, the Murakozi, the Italian Heavy Draught, the Jetland, the Noriker, the North Swedish, the Rhenish-German Heavy, the Lithuanian Heavy Draught, the Russian Heavy Draught, the Vladimir Heavy Draught, the Schleswig-Holstein Heavy, and the Suffolk.

Heavy horses all, each a special breed with their own set of characteristics, ones that endeared them to owners and admirers as well. And each in some way connected to the Clydesdales: whether a direct or distant kin, whether in looks, shape, mannerism, or working abilities.

Of the breeds, it is the Shire, the Percheron, and the Belgian that are of most intrigue to Clydesdale lovers. Each has its own unique characteristics.

Regarding the Percheron (a native of the Perche region of northwest France), it is said, with all due respect to the other breeds, that it may be the most handsome of all the heavy horses. At one time or another, a farm horse, a coach horse, a war-horse, and a riding horse, the Percheron embodies many of the facial features of the Arab breed. Elegant is a word used often to describe the horse that stands between sixteen and nineteen hands high and whose weight approaches a ton (2000 pounds). To gain a bit more reference, a hippopotamus weighs up to 7,000 pounds while an elephant clicks the scales at nearly 15,000 pounds, making Percherons and their heavy horse brethren among the heaviest animals to ever walk the face of the earth save the dinosaur.

Normally black or what is called dappled gray, the Percheron, according to legend, is the model for the dapple-gray rocking horse. With thick mane, a stately head, square forehead, and large eyes, it is distinctive. History has recorded that the breed was instrumental in assisting the efforts of the Franks in administering a beating to the Moslems at the Battle of Poitiers in 732 AD.

In the early years of the nineteenth century, one of the most famous of the Percherons was created when Jean le Blanc, son of Gallipoli, an Arab stallion, arrived at Mauves-sur-Huisne in

Carl Moulton drives his Shire six-horse hitch at the 1993 Live Oak Invitational

Paul Maye drives a Unicorn of Ayrshire Farm Shires on the grounds of Shelburne Farm, Shelburne, Vermont

1830. He became a noted member of the breed, one that enjoyed its limelight, as did others of the heavy horses, from about 1880 to 1920. Many were workhorses during World War I, trudging ahead pulling gun-carts and soldiers through the mud and sludge of the war zones. One famous photograph portrays the poor animals actually being fitted with gas masks to protect them from the poison.

"If any breed of heavy horse can truly be said to have legs like tree trunks, it must surely be the Belgian Heavy Draught." This is the claim by author Valerie Russell in her book, *Heavy Horses of the World*. Speaking about the modern breed (the North American Belgian has developed into a taller horse with much more quality than their European cousins), she also calls the Belgian, "The bulkiest of all the heavies," pointing out that they stand as high as seventeen hands with a weight that passes the one ton mark.

Descending from the ancient Forest Horse of the Ice Age, the Belgian, while presenting an expressive face and a fluffy mane that is parted in the middle, appears to have a bit of the "sinking gut" syndrome triggering a belly that may slope toward the ground. Despite this adversity, the Belgian is a proud animal, as witnessed by two grand champions, Brilliant, who won the International Championship in Paris in 1878, and Jupiter, a champion as well. Breedings included Brin d'Or, a large bay with white markings.

During World War I, the western allies used some Belgians from parts of the country they occupied. The Germans did likewise in Belgium and France. Belgians also played their role in WWII, along with some 20,000 heavy horses. The Russians employed the services of more than a million horses, but probably none of them were Belgians. The breed had first been exported from Europe to America in 1886. According to records, Dr. A. G. Hoorebeke of Illinois cared for the animals.

Belgian Mare Taylor Creek Stic-O-Luck, shown by Bob Whisman, Cicero, Indiana

Paul Sparrow, son of Dick Sparrow, the man behind the Famous Belgian Forty Horse Hitch (as seen on right)

The Belgians became fodder for worldwide headlines in 1972 when a gent named Dick Sparrow created the famous "Forty Horse Hitch" for the Jos. Schlitz Breweries of Milwaukee. The wagon he used was more than twenty-two feet in length, with the horses stretching in front of him more than 100 feet. A newspaper cartoon of the time depicted Sparrow attempting to traverse a corner by yelling to a back horse, "Giddy-Up and Pass It Along."

That the Percherons and the Belgians served in the army was no revelation since the horse had long been a cherished member of the legions. English poet Rudyard Kipling indicated their importance when he said, "Four things greater than all things are—Women and Horses and Power and War." The Clydesdales' part in all this is unclear, but they were certainly suited to carry their weight, so to speak. The *Clydesdales Breed* reported that "Two Clydesdales will do the work of three Shires, and their town life will be double at this class of work, i. e. you only need two Clydesdales to last as long as six Shires." On the back cover, surrounding a photograph of a prized Clyde, was written, "[Clydesdales], a combination of strength, weight, utility, dignity." Tracing the exportation of the Clydesdales from its European origin is noteworthy since it triggered a real sense of contribution by the breed to the world of agriculture. Until the era of mechanization occurred, it was the Clydesdales that pulled the plows to dig up rich earth. Planting could occur and vast acreages of wheat and other agricultural products flourished.

During the late nineteenth and early twentieth centuries, literally thousands of Clydesdales traversed the waters of the Atlantic and other oceans on their way to Canada, the United States, and then to Australia. They were also transported to New Zealand, South Africa, and other countries.

The Canadians were the first North Americans to own Clydesdales, with a Scottish gent named David Rowntree, Jr., of Weston, Ontario a good bet as the very first. He is given credit for importing a stallion named Cumberland, a bay bred in England with a star on his forehead, in the 1840s.

These were welcome visitors to those Scots that had decided to call Canada their home. Along with their horse sense, they contributed their families, the Ayrshire "cews," the heritage of the Presbyterian Church, and the distinctive speech pattern that nails one as being a Scot the moment he or she speaks a word. An outstanding article in The *Draft Horse Journal* article by Maury Telleen called *Six Stallions Who Were Important In the Rebuilding of the Clydesdales Breed In The United States* provided further thought about the impact of the Scots on heavy horses both in Canada and the United States:

"The grooms who came over with those importations also attracted their share of favorable attention. They were the kind of young men, horsemen, and stockmen born to the business that American breeders, importers, and colleges of agriculture were anxious to hire. A good many lads who had grown up with the Clydesdales and shipped over here with them wound up making major contributions to the Percheron and Belgian breeds in our country. Thousands of farm boys 'learned things Dad didn't know' from the many Scots who served as grooms, herdsmen, and shepherds at our great land grant schools."

Shipping the huge animals across the Atlantic was no easy task, with many ships and their precious cargo lost. The voyage took at least five or six weeks, even in good weather, and the sailing ships were thus required to stock feed and water for a lengthy period of time. Besides this expense, freight costs reached $300, a considerable sum in those days.

Cumberland (some Scots resisted the name since it reminded them of the British Battle of Culloden) was followed into Canadian existence by three fellow Clydesdales—Grey Clyde, Sovereign, and Marquis of Clyde. The former, imported by Archibald Ward of Markham, made the most positive impression. In Grant McEwan's book, *Heavy Horses*, he was described as "rich dappled grey with a massive frame, near-perfect feet and legs and a small head."

Lochinvar, Clydesdale Stallion, two-time Grand Champion at Chicago International, 1928 and 1931, owned by J. E. Falconer of Goven, Saskatchewan, Canada

Clydesdales invaded western Canada, with Charming Charlie (foaled in Scotland in 1883) appearing three years later. Imported by Alex Colquhoun of Colquhoun and Beattie, Brandon, the horse's cost was equated to one Canadian currency per horse pound. When they weighed Charming Charlie, "the tab was $2,163" with partner Beattie laughing when "That damn Aberdonian refused to 'knock off' the three dollars." The price proved worthy when Charlie became an undefeated champion, winning his last victory at the age of eleven in Winnipeg.

The first Canadian stud book appeared in 1886, the same year the Clydesdales Association of Canada was formed. A common expression noting the horse's contribution to Canada was, "The Clydesdale made Canada draught [draft] horse conscious and Canada owes it a lasting debt."

No less a man of royalty than the Duke of Windsor, when he was called the Prince of Wales, was a Clydesdale admirer who owned a stud of the breed on a ranch in the vicinity of Calgary. His involvement sparked interest in the Clydesdales until the advent of the motorcar and the tractor. Even as late as 1952, there still were some 140 Clydesdales in competition at the Toronto Fair.

In 1879, the American Clydesdale Association was formed in the United States, an organization that is still a force in the twenty-first century. It celebrated its 125th anniversary in 2004. The association's first entries included such breeders as N. P. Clark from Minnesota, R. B. Oglivie from Wisconsin, the Galbraith brothers of Wisconsin, the Powell Brothers from Pennsylvania, and Colonel Robert Holloway of Illinois.

> ### How much can a Clydesdale horse pull?
> It depends on what they are pulling. When pulling a wagon, a Clydesdale can pull many times more than its own weight. This is why the Clydesdale was so popular in the cities where it pulled large wagons packed with goods.

Many believe that the very first Clydesdale in the United States may have been the formidable Grey Clyde, first owned, as stated, by Archibald Ward. In 1848, he sold the gallant horse to Joseph Thompson of Columbus, Ontario. Shown at the New York State Fair in Buffalo in 1848, he won first prize in his class.

In the fall of 1851, Grey Clyde was sold to Kilgour and Cushman of Mason County, Kentucky but was not delivered until the spring. He died in October 1852.

The Canadian influence on American Clydesdales is bolstered by the exploits of a true pioneer named Alexander Galbraith, dubbed The Horseman's Horseman. He was the son of Alex Galbraith, a very successful Clyde breeder and stallion owner from Croy, Cunningham, Kilearn, Scotland. He and his brothers journeyed abroad to Janesville, Wisconsin in 1881 to open an English horse importing business. This proved successful with the first to be imported the son of the famous Prince of Wales, Glencoe.

Clydesdales from the 1800s

In the 1888 *Breeder's Gazette*, the Galbraiths advertised 150 stallions, including Clydesdales, Shires, Hackneys, and Cleveland Bays. In the December issue, nearly 200 were advertised. Unfortunately, the depression of 1892 ruined the Galbraith import venture, and Alex's two brothers returned to Scotland.

Over the years, young Alex, also the breeder of English sheep dogs, was the premier trader of horses, a trend that continued again at the turn of the twentieth century when economic times caused a halt to his exploits. He farmed for a bit, but was then back with the animals he loved in connection with educational programs at the University of Wisconsin in nearby Madison. With his son, he worked both sides of the border, becoming an expert called upon to judge competitions in both Canada and the United States. He also established a stable in Brandon, Manitoba and another in Edmonton, Alberta.

As a tribute to Galbraith, De Witt Wing, associate editor of the *Breeder's Gazette*, wrote that Alex possessed, "Distinctive courtesy, scrupulous conscientiousness, unswerving loyalties, and a clean serene life."

Top Canadian Clydesdale importers included Robert Beith, D. and O. Sorby, and the Graham brothers: Robert, Tom, and William. All were from Ontario. In 1910, while U.S. imports continued to lag, Canadian imports from Scotland reached more than 1300. World War I and the invention of the tractor dimmed the number of imports, but Clydesdales continued to cross the ocean to America.

Two important breeders in Canadian history were: Ben Finlayson, born in Perthshire, Scotland and called by author MacEwan, "A superb judge of heavy horses and, if anything, a better showman than a judge"; and W. H. "Scotty" Bryce of Arcola, Saskatchewan. The former landed in Brandon, Manitoba and began importing on a large scale. He was responsible for importing from Scotland ten of the seventeen stallion champions at the Toronto Royal Agricultural Winter Fair before World War II. They were First Principal (1922), Arnprior Emigrant (1924, 1926, and 1929), Sansovino (1930), and Lochinvar (1928, 1931, 1933, 1935, and 1936).

Bryce became a legend in the Canadian Clydesdale world when James Kilpatrick, the recognized number one expert in the world

Alex Galbraith driving the Hickory Springs Farm/Parker Taft Hitch of Freeport, Illinois during the 1959 International Livestock Expo

The gelding team of Bullet and Stricker owned by David Stalhiem bind corn on his farm in Amery, Wisconsin

on the breed, arrived from Scotland in 1912. Owner of Craigie Mains, a legendary Scottish Clydesdale farm, he called Arcola's stable of horses, "the best stud Clydesdales in Canada." They had been part of a group of twelve imported in 1905, including Rosadora and Perpetual Motion.

The most significant Canadian breeder after World War II was Ontario's Wreford Hewson. His Clydesdales dominated the Royal Agricultural Winter Fair for nearly thirty years. His Bardrill Castle left his bloodline imprint on the American scene with championship showings in the 1960s, 1970s, and 1980s.

In Australia, the Clydesdales earned the labels "the breed that built Australia" and "the unsung heroes of the outback." As described in *Heavy Horses of the World* by Valerie Russell, "In appalling conditions of drought, flood, and dust storms, they hauled stores, timber, wool, wheat and minerals; they helped construct the roads and the giant tanks or dams to store precious water; and they pulled the ploughs that dug the drains to carry that scarce commodity through the parched country of the 'back-blocks.'"

According to the publication The *Clydesdales Breed*, "The State of Victoria, and the Province of Otago [New Zealand] in particular, got many very high-class horses and mares, and in 1883 a choice shipment was made to Queensland."

Commenting on the type of Clydesdales suitable down under, Archibald MacNeilage, editor of The *Scottish Farmer* in the early 1900s, said, "It should never be overlooked that Australia must, for climatic reasons, have horses with more bone and hair than would be deemed necessary in this country. Horses soon lose the characteristics of plenty of hair and big bone under the climatic conditions of Australia."

Around 1880, the Clydesdale began to appear on the docks, and farmers immediately purchased the animals to work their labor in the wheat fields of Victoria. Eight to ten horse teams roamed the acreage, oftentimes with a plough complete with seat behind them. Many times the horses would be sixteen in number—they were never reigned—only controlled by the farmer's mouth. This continued until the 1920s when the tractor began to appear, but when tractors became too expensive, the Clydesdales were there to save the day. One of the outstanding Clydesdales exported to Australia from Scotland was Flashdale. He won the well-regarded Cawdor Cup in 1923.

While the Clydesdales made their presence known in Canada and Australia, their evolution in the United States was fast arriving. Land needed to be cleared for cultivation, and the heavy horses were perfect choices to remove stumps, boulders, and logs. Horse-drawn wagons and carts appeared to transport manufactured goods and crops, and wagon trains were utilized to move families and their belongings through rigorous territory. Nineteenth-century cities featured horse-drawn trolleys. Many a vehicle was pulled by heavy horses.

Chief among the contributors to the prominence of the breed was the famous Colonel Holloway of Alexis, Illinois. He was known as a "southern gentleman" whose ownership of a Scottish Clydesdale named Cedric was part of horse folklore.

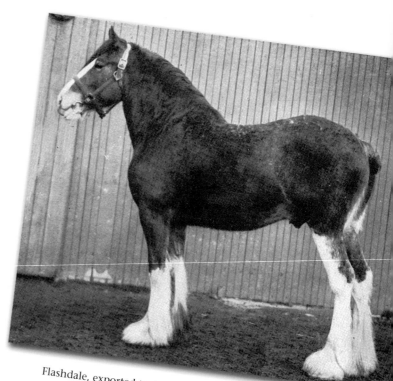

Flashdale, exported to Australia where he did tireless work as a sire

The dam of the horse was owned by Dr. James McCall of Gallowhill (near Glasgow). After a successful operation to cure an infectious condition called "Poll evil," she was mated to Merryton Prince of Wales. Cedric was the result of this courtship in 1875.

After being sold to another, Cedric was sent to the United States where the Colonel spied him, and a trade was finalized. The purchase turned out to be a wise one since Cedric was a coveted sire whose offspring included fourteen stallions shipped back to Scotland by Andrew and William Montgomery of Netherhall and Banks, Kirkcudbright, at the time the most prominent Clydesdale stud owner in Scotland.

Handsome Prince

> ### How much do Clydesdales eat?
>
> Depending on their age and the amount of work they are doing, adult Clydesdales may eat 25 to 50 pounds of hay and 2 to 10 pounds of grain or other supplements a day.

If these men constitute the true pioneers of the Clydesdale influence in the United States, there is a second tier of those that continued the tradition. Among them were A. G. Soderberg, Osco, Illinois; G. A. Cluett

Across the state line in Wisconsin, R. B. Ogilvie owned a Clydesdales Stud at Blarigowerie Farm. His star pupil was McQueen, a stallion unbeaten in competition. Later to become the secretary of the breeder's association, Ogilvie was well-known for his knowledge of Clydesdales and for his outstanding character.

Fellow Wisconsin residents, the McLay brothers of Janesville, became prominent around the turn of the twentieth century when they purchased one of Cedric's offspring, a bred stallion named Handsome Prince. N. P. Clark, St. Cloud, Minnesota wanted so badly to win the 1893 World's Fair that he contacted William Montgomery in Scotland and purchased Prince Patrick. He was victorious with two Cedric sons, Prince of Quality and Handsome Prince, second and third.

Alex Galbraith, along with his employee, "Uncle John" Smith, arranged for sixty stallions to be shipped from Scotland to Wisconsin. Some were sold in western Canada, with others shipped to Oregon and Washington as the Clydesdales began to be influential across the country.

A statue in tribute to the Clydesdale, the horse that built Australia

of Williamstown, Massachusetts; Robert A. Fairbairn, Newmarket, New Jersey; F. L. Ames, North Easton, Massachusetts; Walter L. Houser, Mondovi, Wisconsin; Eben A. Jones, Bangor, Wisconsin; and John Leitch, Lafayette, Illinois.

By way of Scotland and Canada, the Clydesdales in America emerged as a premier heavy horse. At the 1900 International Exposition, the breed earned prominence in the draft horse classes. Over the next twenty years, they would become even more popular, their gallantry a staple in fields across America.

Harviestoun Baroness, owned by Robert A. Fairbairn of Newmarket, New Jersey

Cedric Princess, winner of the Cawdor Cup in 1903. Cedric's daughter Fickle Fortune Princess was dam of Cedric Princess

Seven-year-old Clydesdale geldings, Wally and Bob, owned by Dr. Chuck Hansell of Columbus, Wisconsin

"And the hoofs of the horses as they run shakes the crumbling field."

—Virgil,
The Aeneid

The American Clydesdales 1900 - 1940

Six-horse hitch of roan Clydesdales created by Stevenson's and Sons Funeral Home and J.R. and Diann Grierson both of Miles City, Montana for the 1998 Milwaukee Circus Parade
Ron Johnson doing the driving with Dan Johnson Assisting

In 1892, the first National Clydesdales Sale was organized. Seventy-seven stallions and mares were sold, with top dollar being $900 for the best stallion and $450 for the mare. Over the years from 1900 to 1920, these prices would increase in accordance with the escalating popularity of the wondrous horse.

And escalate it did, by such magnitude that it is difficult to imagine. From the few imported just fifty years earlier, registrations (according to state requirements for stallions to be licensed if standing at stud for public service) jumped to more than 21,000 from 1892 to 1920.

Most important, the number of imported Clydesdales shrunk as U.S. breeders became as competent as the Scots were. From 1911 to 1920, less than 500 Clydesdales were brought from overseas to America.

The surge of interest in the Clydesdales coincided with agricultural links to the animals. In 1903, there were more than thirty-eight colleges with a draft horse program, and nearly a third featured Clydesdales. Since much of the early breeding had taken place in Wisconsin, it was only fitting that their state university led the way with a pure bred program.

As stated, the 1900 International Livestock Show in Chicago was a breakthrough moment for the Clydesdales. By dominating the inter-breed hitch competition, they took center stage. Packing companies sponsored many of the entries, with the Nelson Morris organization leading the way with seven hitch championships from 1901 to 1910.

It was modern invention of the tractor that really took its toll on the Clydesdale breed. One of the culprits was the Fordson

Bolger Dairy Farms Hitch at the 1959 International Livestock Expo

Model F tractor that appeared in 1917. Smaller in size that many of its predecessors, it was sold at a low cost attractive to the average farmer.

Registrations of Clydesdales dipped in the 1920s to about 200 per year, with the twenty-year period from 1921 to 1941 totaling only 4000. In keeping with the trend, few Clydesdales were imported.

In the mid-1920s, the useful purposes for the Clydesdales had depreciated and the average cost of a good draft horse was around $250, lowered from a high of $725 in 1916. Tractors were rapidly replacing horses for farm work, and by 1930 the agricultural census estimated that the number of purebred Clydesdales on U.S. farms was less than 1500.

A renaissance of sorts occurred in the 1930s when Clydesdale breeders nearly doubled. They could be located in 26 states with Iowa being at the forefront. Farmers turned to tractors to save their crops, and the heavy horses had difficulty recapturing their jobs.

The advent of rubber tires made a difference as well as the tractor and became a staple at nearly every farm. Many of the Clydesdales became window dressing, lounging in the pastures as the tractor engines labored noisily near by.

Wilson Six-Horse Hitch of Clydesdales

The Internationally Famous Six-Horse Hitch of Clydesdales owned by Wilson & Co. Meat Packers, Chicago, Illinois

When World War II broke out, mechanization was the call of the day. To support the troops, crops were needed presto and the tractor was much faster than any horse had ever been when it came to bringing in the crops. Those that put horses on the market during the 1940s could expect little in return.

Wilson Six-Horse Hitch receiving award at Central States Fair 1931

Attending the first lighting of the new Anheuser-Busch electric spectacular in New York City's Times Square are (L to R) August A. Busch Jr., Walt Brady, and Mrs. August A. Busch Jr. (August Bush III's mother). The Dalmatian's name is unknown

If the workload for Clydesdales had diminished, the exhibition of the gallant animals had not. Until the end of the 1920s, the number of entries in international competitions remained strong. Breeders, not companies, constituted most of the competitors. When the 1930s appeared, the interest in competition declined.

Uncle Sam took the wind out of the national organization when tax laws in Illinois were altered. In 1933, the newly formed American Clydesdale Breeders Association re-emerged and was stronger than ever.

This same year, an unforeseen development occurred that would boost the spirits of those who loved their Clydesdales regardless of their faltering popularity as work and show animals. In St. Louis, Missouri, two young men, Adolphus Busch III and August A. (Gussie) Busch, Jr., had decided on a present to cheer up the spirits of their father, August A. Busch, Sr., whose health was failing. It was a present that would change the perception of Clydesdales forever.

The gift was a traditional brewery beer wagon and team of Clydesdales. Soon they would be the showcase for the breed, providing much needed exposure.

Despite the emergence of the Budweiser team, the decline in the popularity of Clydesdales continued. A report in 1936 stated that more than 700,000 horses, a good many of

Anheuser-Busch Clydesdales Six-Horse hitch 1934

Goebel Brewing Co. six-horse hitch with Fred Robinson driving

them Clydesdales, had been displaced from the land. Within ten years, nearly 20,000 tons of horsemeat had been exported to Europe.

For the next two decades, well into the 1960s, there was little market for the horses. In the 1950s and 1960s, less than 1000 Clydesdales were registered. After World War II, most of the competitions ceased to exist. Worse, many of the Clydesdales were shipped off to packing houses, and at one point the American Clydesdale, as it was known, was nearly extinct. Only the efforts of several individuals and families, including Chester Weston, Concord, Michigan; Frank S. Martin, Plymouth, Indiana; Charles Wilhoit, Batavia, Iowa; Nathan Goff, Clarksburg, West Virginia; Floyd Jones and Sons, Bangor, Wisconsin; the Raymond Emmons family, Galesville, Wisconsin; the Grayson Brooks family, Sparta, Wisconsin; P. T. Brown and Sons, Tangier, Indiana; the Fred and Edward Clausen family, Gladbrook, Iowa; the Fred and Fred Polinder, Jr., family, Lynden, Washington; the Harry Castagnasso family, Sonoma, California; and the Bert and Glen Thurston family, Morgan, Utah kept the breed lines alive. Even with their interest, it would take imports from Scotland and Canada to re-establish the horse's existence.

Not that August Busch, Jr., wasn't doing his part. In 1940, he purchased eleven Clydesdales from Scotland, but the ship carrying them was torpedoed and sunk by the Germans.

Anheuser-Busch team in Washington, D.C. 1949

Undaunted, in 1953, based on the continuing success of the Budweiser team, he decided to breed them at Grant's Farm located on the Busch family estate. He purchased stallions and mares from Scotland and Canada, ten in all in 1955, and began to make his mark in the breeding business.

Despite his efforts, the year 1957 was the leanest for Clydesdales in history. Three years later, there were only 34 Clydesdales registered by the Clydesdale Breeders of the United States. The next year, the number was eighteen, and in successive years through 1981, registered Clydesdales never reached the 200 mark with only 54 registered in 1970.

Were the Clydesdales about to become extinct, a forgotten animal on the American scene? Was the legend about to end?

A/B with outdoor advertising 1949

Parade of champions at Chicago International Livestock Expo - 1948

The World's Most Magical Horse

"Horse: A neighing quadruped, used in war, and draught and carriage."

— Samuel Johnson,
*Dictionary of the
English Language*

Saving The Clydesdales

Two Clydesdales say hello at Grant's Farm in St. Louis

Owl Creek Clydesdales in Milwaukee Circus Parade

A circus parade, a noteworthy publication, and the continued existence of a band of Clydesdales sponsored by a national brewery.

The combination of these three, plus a handful of dedicated breeders, would prove to be the savior of the vaunted Clydesdales as the world passed the halfway point of the twentieth century. Without the Milwaukee Circus Parade, the emergence of the *Draft Horse Journal*, and the dedication of August Busch, Jr., to preserving his ever-famous Budweiser team, Clydesdales might have disappeared from view.

The parade was the brainchild of C. P. "Chappie" Fox, a smiling gent who wore black horn-rimmed glasses and a brim-up brown fedora. A member of the state historical society, he was the founder and curator of the Circus World Museum in Baraboo, Wisconsin. It featured restored rare circus wagons of all shapes and sizes.

How much do Clydesdales cost?

Clydesdales vary in price based on many factors—bloodline, quality, size, age, color, and markings. Some Clydesdales may sell for as little as $1000, but most Clydesdales sell for between $2500 and $5000. The top-level horses sell for prices equivalent to luxury automobiles!

Together with Ben Barkin, a Milwaukee public relations expert, Fox dreamed of an old-fashioned circus parade that would showcase the circus wagons. His dream turned into an internationally famous July event featuring more than 300 draft horses and 400 riding horses and ponies. During the parade, first held in Milwaukee on July 4, 1963, visitors could see the Snake Den Wagon built by Ringling Bros. Circus in the early 1900s and the 1903 Hemisphere Wagon, at twenty-eight feet the world's largest bandwagon.

From the beginning, the pageantry of the event was colorful and horse-lovers from all over the globe cheered their favorite breed in a re-creation of the circus street parades of old.

Twenty-five wagons from the museum were drawn by Clydesdales, Belgians, and Percherons. Representing the Clydesdales, according to an article in the 2003 Clydesdale News, were eight horse hitches from Bolger Dairy, Hawthorn-Mellody Dairy, and Parker Taft of Freeport, Illinois. Six horse hitches were presented by Melvin Lietzke and Erick Struck, Floyd Jones and Ray Emmons.

Ray Emmons's son Jim, a noted Clydesdale expert and a top breeder to boot, recalls his first impression of the Milwaukee parade. "There were more good horses than I had ever seen before," he said. "Something very special."

While the first issue of *The Draft Horse Journal* appeared in the spring of 1964, the fall issue, published in August, promoted the parade. On the cover was a photograph of an eight horse Clydesdale hitch (owned by Parker Taft) on a paved street with hundreds of onlookers watching with admiration. Underneath the photograph was printed, "Belgian - Clydesdale - Percheron - Shire - Suffolk."

Founded and edited by Maury Telleen, the importance of *The Draft Horse Journal*, a publication featuring every aspect of heavy horses, was documented in the 1986 *Clydesdale News*, a publication of the Clydesdale Breeders of the U.S.A. In an article titled, "They Tell It to the Telleens—Story of the Draft Horse Journal," author Patrick O'Sheel writes, "Back in 1964, the market for draft horses in America was near death's door. By the logic of Progress, the big breeds were finished. Starting up the Journal looked like an act of radical enthusiasm and innocence. But not quite innocence, considering that Maury Telleen was then in his fourth year as manager of the National Dairy Congress. He thus knew many of the stubborn farmers who had hung on to their horses through the great sell-off." Later in the article, O'Sheel added, "one whimsical breeder hailed the editor [Telleen] as a 'Moses leading the draft horse people out of the wilderness.'"

All the while, the Budweiser Clydesdale team continued to gain prominence. Beginning with the early days of television, commercials touting the Bud wagon and the Clydesdales promoted beer. A catchy jingle accompanied the image of the Clydesdales, decorated in bright red and white as they trotted down a remote road. In the winter, a snow-covered scene was prevalent. In spring, the summer, and the fall, the animals could be seen in serene settings depicting their calm and grace.

To be certain, the Clydesdales had become a respected symbol of corporate products, an identification that the Anheuser-Busch brewery relished. The fact that twenty-two more

Ray Emmons and Emminent's Fritz, Reserve Grand Champion, at the 1961 National Show in Des Moines, Iowa

Clydesdales were imported from Scotland along with several mares from Canada told the story—the commercials were selling beer, and a great deal of it. By 1966, Anheuser-Busch had the largest Clydesdale breeding herd in the country.

The Budweiser Clydesdales phenomenon began as mentioned, oddly enough, during the Prohibition Era in late 1932 when Adolphus Busch III and August A. (Gussie) Busch, Jr., the sons of August A. Busch, Sr., purchased a brewery beer wagon and sixteen Clydesdales as a present for their ailing father. The brewery wagon was an old one in storage that was repainted red with white trim. The sons could have chosen any of the heavy horses, but August A. Busch, Jr., learned that several Clydesdales were available at the Union Stock Yards in Chicago. His reasoning included the belief that the "Clydesdales were unquestionably the showiest and would make an impressive team."

The sons, with the approval of the company's board of directors, recruited two of the company's teamsters, Art Zerr and Billy Wales, to train the new hitches. In late March 1933, the surprise was ready to be sprung on August A. Busch, Sr.

On a bright, spring day with the flowers blooming around the St. Louis area, August Busch, Jr., asked his father to walk outside and see his new "vehicle." Believing that his son had wasted money on another spanking new Pierce-Arrow, Busch, Sr., began to berate Junior for being a spendthrift when prohibition wasn't over.

Draft Horse Journal Cover Spring, 2002

When Papa Busch walked out of the Old Schoolhouse, he couldn't believe his eyes as he spied six wondrous Clydesdales in lock step pulling the shiny new wagon down Pestalozzi Street. Emotions caused him to shed a tear or two as the sons relished the moment with their father.

Seizing the opportunity to use the Clydesdale team to advantage once Prohibition ended, the decision was made to reintroduce the Budweiser brand to beer drinkers by having two teams travel: one to Chicago and the other to the East Coast so that the brewery could thank government officials instrumental in repealing Prohibition.

At midnight on April 7, 1933, Prohibition ended. When cases of beer were ready for transportation, Eberhard Anheuser II, grandson of the brewery's co-founder, boarded a TWA Ford Tri-Motor airplane at St. Louis's Lambert Field for a flight to Newark, New Jersey. The beer was unloaded on the wagons previously shipped by train along with the Clydesdales. The hitch then traveled through the Holland Tunnel to the Empire State Building at Fifth Avenue and 34th Street. A crowd of more than five thousand onlookers gathered as former New York Governor and unsuccessful Presidential candidate Al Smith, a longtime supporter of repeal, received his case of freshly-brewed Budweiser.

After a publicity-boosting appearance in the Big Apple, the hitch team visited Philadelphia, Hartford, Boston, Providence,

"Bringing you something more" advertisement for Anheuser-Busch

and Washington D.C. There the first case of Bud to be brewed from the production line was delivered to President Franklin D. Roosevelt, who had led the fight for the repeal of Prohibition. In St. Louis, the brewery received hundreds of letters and telephone calls from people thanking Anheuser-Busch for sending the Clydesdale hitch team to their city. According to the brewery historian, "They remarked how seeing the hitch reminded them of earlier, better days before Prohibition and motorized trucks when beer wagons, and other horse drawn vehicles, were a common sight on the streets."

Anheuser-Busch Eight-Horse Hitch at Union Stock Yards

This exposure and the ensuing tours of the hitch team that reached more than eighty cities across the U.S.A. not only boosted the image of the brewery and its beer, but also provided a much-needed nudge for the Clydesdales into the limelight. As John Zawadzki, the Scottish expert says, "The Budweiser horses became the standard for Clydesdales."

The importance of the contribution by Anheuser-Busch cannot be underestimated. With the exception of a handful of dedicated breeders, interest in the breed had died, and it was only through the continued exposure of the grand horses that the public continued to be aware they existed. Berry Farrell, the breeding farm manager beginning in 1969 and a noted expert on the breed, says in *All The Kings Horses*, "If it hadn't been for Mr. Busch's support, Clydesdales wouldn't have survived in the United States. He encouraged their breeding at a time when few other people had the interest or the resources to do so."

Besides gaining much needed exposure for the breed (and for Dalmatians who began to accompany the Clydesdales as early as 1950), the brewery added to the surge of reconnecting the Clydesdales to the public by sponsoring awards, including the August Busch, Jr., Award, at the National Clydesdale Show. Competitions at Waterloo, Iowa and the Ohio, Indiana, Michigan, and Wisconsin state fairs added zest to the quest to re-establish the prominence of the Clydesdale.

The Open House and Production Sale at Grant's Farm in St. Louis, sponsored by Anheuser-Busch, brought more than 200 Clydesdale lovers to the city in May 1970. A sale was held and twenty-one top horses were sold, many to enthusiasts in different parts of the country adding new breeding areas to the mix. August Busch, Jr., also gave away a yearling stallion and a yearling filly and offered free breeding to their most prized stallions through a letter he wrote dated January 21, 1970 when the popularity of the breed was at a low point. In part it read, "To preserve and promote this fine breed, Anheuser-Busch, Inc. is offering the services of its Clydesdale stallions to other Clydesdale owners in the United States and Canada for free stud service."

Anheuser-Busch representative John Maier presents a case of Budweiser to former New York Governor Al Smith shortly after repeal of Prohibition

August A. Busch Jr. waves to the crowd on the 50th anniversary of the introduction of the Clydesdale hitch (April, 7 1983). Along side him is driver Ned Niemiec and unidentified man

Anheuser-Busch 6-horse hitch in New York repeal

The importance of this offer was emphasized in an article in the Autumn 2004 *Draft Horse Journal*. In part, it read, "[The Budweiser offer] . . . gave many breeders access to quality stallions and a number of good horses resulted from this offer that might otherwise never have been conceived."

By the 1970s, Clydesdales had regained their popularity as evidenced by the fact that they were being sold for more than two thousand dollars each. Anheuser-Busch celebrated its continuing love for the animal and its commercials by producing a thirty-minute documentary in 1983 called *All The Kings Horses*. Today, millions of people can witness the legend of the Clydesdales by visiting Grant's Farm and the Budweiser brewing facility in St. Louis where the majestic poise and power of the breed is on display. A glimpse of them can also be seen at other Budweiser locations including those located at Sea World of California, Sea World of Texas, Sea World of Florida, and Busch Gardens in Tampa, Florida.

August A. Busch, Jr. Memorial Trophy Winner Pinnacle's Lady Jane owned by Linda-Harmon Dodge

The first National Clydesdale Show was held at the Iowa State Fair in 1961. Bardrill Blackie, owned by Packer Taft of Freeport, Illinois, was the Grand Champion Mare. Taft also placed his Six Horse Hitch second to Anhueser-Busch.

After the show was held in DuQuoin, Illinois for a year, it was hosted for the next four years at the Michigan State Fair in Detroit. Waterloo, Iowa had the show at the Diary Cattle Congress for the next five years, with the show being held at the Ohio State Fair in 1973 until it returned to Waterloo in 1974.

In 1975, the National Show moved to the Wisconsin State Fair in Milwaukee where Floyd and Dan Jones dominated, winning both Grand Champions and Top Gelding prize as well as finishing second in the Clydes Six Horse Hitch to the Northumberland Clydes owned by the Emmons family of Galesville, Wisconsin. Other prestigious exhibitors at this show included P. T. Brown and Sons, Tangier, Indiana; Lloyd and Phyllis Paul, Roanoke, Indiana; Richard Wegner, Clinton, Michigan; James and Betty Groves, Pecatonica, Illinois; Dale Brasel, Milford, Illinois; and Dr. Ralph Schwartz, Darlington, Wisconsin.

Indicative of the renewed popularity of the breed, 162 horses sold at prices averaging over thirty-nine hundred dollars during the 2004 sale, with some selling for more than $20,000. Top seller was Lady Kassy of Grandview owned by Daryl and Lorraine Cobbs of Huntington, Indiana. She sold for $22,000.

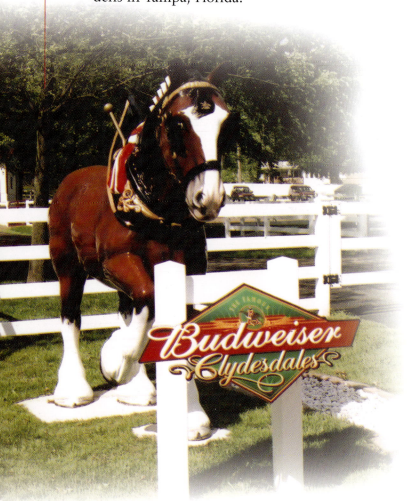

Grant's Farm Statue as tribute to the Clydesdale

During the 1980s, a "Clydesdale Store" was established by the breeders association to promote Clydes through the sale of various items. In 1999, an important step was taken when the Clydesdales Education

Bardrill Glenord, Grand Champion, Toronto Royal Agricultural Winter Fair Five Times

Foundation was finalized. Its purpose is "to provide cultural, historical, and educational information about the Clydesdale horse, and to conduct studies, instruction, training, and research for the continuous growth and perpetuation of the Clydesdale horse."

The cooperative effort to save Clydesdales, a breed that bordered on extinction, continues. As the calendar turned to the twenty-first century, more than 900 members belonged to the Clydesdale Breeders' of the U.S.A., with yearly registrations exceeding 600 and over 700 Clydesdales transferring to new ownership annually.

As the question of whether the Clydesdales would slowly slip from view had hovered over the industry, several of the breed were more critical to its survival than others. In the article, *Six Stallions Who Were Important In The Rebuilding Of the Clydesdales Breed In The United States*, written by Maury Telleen in *The Draft Horse Journal*, he proposes that it was Balgreen Final Command, Masterman, Bardrill Glenord, Dunsyre Silver King, Doura Excelsior, and Master Baron who, more than any others, kept the Clydesdale dream alive.

Of these, Balgreen Final Command, bred by Robert Donald of Ballochmorrie of Ayrshire, Scotland, was, according to expert Berry Farrell, "One of the all-time best Clydesdale stallions. So many of our top horses of today trace to him twice or more. He had the ability to sire top show stock, top breeding stock, and top hitch horses . . ."

Paul Cooper, a top breeder, added in the article, "The potential of this horse was recognized almost immediately. As a yearling he was considered the truest Clydesdale type to appear up to that date and was acclaimed as a type model. His impact was such that he won the Cawdor Cup in 1944, the first yearling colt to win that distinguished award at the Stallion Show. Called 'the father of his country' by author Telleen, he won the Daniel Gardner Memorial Cup at the Glasgow Stallion Show that year." In Scotland, the horse's prowess was felt through two favored sons, Dunsyre

Aged Mares at the 1969 National Show in Waterloo, Iowa, led by the Grand Champion Mare Leading Lady of Belleau owned by Floyd Conger and Jim and Betty Groves

Footprint and Salchrie Prince Philip. Another was Dunsyre Hiawatha, imported into Canada.

Balgreen Final Command was imported in the summer of 1955. He sired five daughters that would be Grand Champions at the Wisconsin State Fair, the largest Clydesdale show in the United States at the time.

Another son, Commander, was sired in Scotland, and imported to Canada by Nile Shantz. He later joined the Budweiser team and for fifteen years became a "high-stepping, forceful lead horse in that great hitch."

Dunsyre Silver King, bred by Alexander Allison of Lanarkshire, Scotland, was foaled on April 20, 1958. Regarding him, Berry Ferrell stated, "King had a terrific pedigree. Not only was he a double grandson of Dunsyre Footprint - probably the best breeding horse by old Final Command - but the dams in his pedigree were powerful matrons . . . To show you how much we thought of him, we had 16 Silver King daughters in the herd at one time." Author Telleen added, "Silver King left 54 registered offspring in our American stud book. Allowing for foals that died and horse colts not registered, that is a fair number for a Clydesdale in America. I think he played an important part in rebuilding the breed here in the U.S. Dunsyre Silver King is obviously a case where 'pedigree meant something.' He came from good stock and left good stock." One offspring was daughter Belleau Flower Girl, described by Ed Henken, past president of the Clydesdale Breeders of the United States, as

(L to R) Clydesdale Breeders of the USA secretary Betty Groves' son Randy poses with Clydesdale Breeders of the USA board member Lisa Banga, Anheuser-Busch director of operations Jim Poole and his wife Marie

Balgreen Final Command

"a powerful mare that stood an honest 18 hands on unexcelled feet 10 to 11 inches wide, both front and hind, measured while unshod and in the pasture. She was a splendid mover and could lead a hitch if you could find enough big horses to go behind her."

Berry Farrell described Bardrill Glenord as having "a beautiful flat bone and plenty of it. He had plenty of beautiful silky feather, a lot of body, a great hoofhead, and foot plus faultless action . . . but best of all he had a wonderful disposition. You could breed a mare with him with nothing more than a baler twine on his halter." Over the years, Bardrill Glenord would contribute twenty-one sons to the Budweiser hitches.

Doura Excelsior was born in 1964 in Lincolnshire, located in the southern area of Great Britain. Parke Brown of Tangier, Indiana and former president of the Clydesdale Breeders of the U.S.A. said, "Excelsior was bred in the purple. His sire, Salchrie Prince Phillip, was one of the first offspring of the high respected Balgree Final Command, while his dam was a granddaughter of Craigie Beau Ideal, called by the master breeder James Kilpatrick, the greatest stallion he ever owned."

In 1967, Excelsior won both the Cawdor Cup and Medcalf Cup. He was called "the best 3-year-old ever exhibited in Scotland." Two years later, an Excelsior filly foal, Kirklandhill Queen O'Carrick, won the Cawdor Cup for females and then was sold to Wreford Hewson of Ontario.

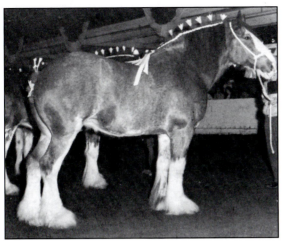

Queen O' Carrick

Masterman

Queen O'Carrick was Grand Champion Mare of the Royal Agricultural Winter Fair a record fourteen times. She stood Reserve Grand Champion three times.

Author Maury Telleen stated, "The prepotency of Excelsior during the reign of 'Queen O'Carrick' was demonstrated many times in that ring in Toronto. On two occasions when Queen O'Carrick took Supreme honors, her own half sisters, led into the ring by Paul Cooper of Mukwanago, Wisconsin, took reserve honors. In all, Excelsior sired eight Cawdor Cup champions."

Paul Cooper was a huge admirer of Excelsior. "[He] was not a big horse but was loaded well with quality. He had a beautiful hind leg, feather, top line and head . . . He was the most intelligent horse I have ever seen. The most impressive feat occurred the first time I saw him. I was eager to see him move and asked Mr. Jim Young to bring him out. The horse knew what to do. He waited for me to get behind him, and then took two or three walking steps. He then moved into a trot at the correct speed for him, went about 90 feet, made the proper Scottish turn, and trotted back. He then set up perfectly, head in the air, ears pointed attentively. He stayed that way until the lead was strapped on again."

> ### May Clydesdales be ridden?
>
> Yes! Most equipment manufacturers now offer saddles, bits, and bridles in draft horse sizes. Many owners compete in shows next to more typical riding horses. The Clydesdales are very easy to train and their great style is a hit in the show ring. They also make exceptional trail horses due to their calm disposition.

Another contributor to the revitalization of the Clydesdales in America was Masterman by Bardrill Castle, foaled in 1961 at the stable of Wreford Hewson in Ontario. Berry Farrell describes Masterman as follows: "He was not a big horse by today's standards. He was a little different in type than his counterparts here in the stallion barn. He had an extremely nice hind leg, a mover . . . He was a sire of harness horses. I have never seen a Masterman son or daughter that could not wear the harness well. They were stylish movers with lots of 'go.'"

Masterman was responsible for fifty-one registered offspring. Presented to Texas A&M as a research project, he showed his firepower by jumping a fence and breeding with two quarter horse mares. Among his prized children were Belleau Master Joe, Belleau Refiner's Lady, Belleau Gina, and Belleau Miss Masterman, a Budweiser performer. When Walt Brady, a featured driver for Bud for many years, died, it was Pete, son of Masterman and a lead horse at the time, who was selected to be at the funeral.

Any re-establishment of the Clydesdale breed in the West can be directly attributed to Master Baron by Bardrill Castle, called "a Garth Brooks type of stallion, a country boy," by author Telleen. Berry Farrell said, "Anyone who saw Master Baron could not help being impressed with the amount of feather he possessed. At the time the Thurstons [Glen Thurston, Morgan, Utah] got him, their mares were somewhat lacking in feather and he put the feather back in the foals. Color-wise, he was right for his time. Master Baron was a beautiful rich bay that quickly took the eye of horsemen, and non-horsemen alike." Ed Henken adds, "He developed into an exceptionally thick horse of great weight and substance. His solid bay coat, with blaze and four white stockings, together with his soundness and draftiness, met all the requirements of the demanding Rocky Mountain breeders." Sons included Baron's Buddy, shown at the Grand Championships in 1974 by Jim and Betty Groves. Later, he was sold to Anheuser Busch.

Master Baron with Mrs. Dale Thurston at the halter

Armageddon's Lord Reuben

Another son was Dandy John, known as "Johnny." Yet another son, T. H. V. Hexy, sired many large geldings for Budweiser.

In the modern era, several outstanding Clydesdales have appeared at the top shows, including Toronto, Milwaukee, Indianapolis, Lansing, Michigan, and Springfield, Illinois. Among them has been Live Oak Grandeur by Doura Sensation whose mother was Northumberland Melinda. Credentials include three Grand Champion trophies at the National Clydesdale show, and twice Grand Champion at The Royal Agricultural Winter Fair in Toronto.

Outstanding Clydesdales since the early 1990s include Northwest Glenord's Shea, owned by Bill and Sharon Dean of Ortonville, Michigan and bred by Edwin Henken of Ferndale, Washington. He was the Grand Champion Stallion in 1991 and also Grand Champion at the Toronto Royal Agricultural Winter Fair in 1993, the first American Clydesdale to win that high honor since Green Meadow Footstep won in 1925.

Dr. John and Charlotte Weber of Ocala, Florida were successful that year as well, with Hillmoor Rosette by Ayton Perfection becoming Grand Champion Mare at both the Milwaukee show and in Toronto. The Weber's Six Horse Hitch driven by Jim Westbrook won the National in both 1991 and 1992.

Additional champion Clydesdales during the early 1990s included Hillmoor Fusilier by Ayton Perfection and Thislle Ridge Argyll Fancy owned by David and Wilma Cleghorn of Ariss, Ontario; Armageddon's Lord Elijah, owned by The Cobbs family of Huntington, Indiana and bred by Dr. Michael and Cheri Moleski, who also bred Armageddon's Mistress Eve by Solomon's Commander, a Grand Champion mare; and CIE Perfection and CIE Champagne Lady, full brother and sister, Grand Champions in 1993 and owned by Gene Cooper. Their dam was Doura Douglas Delight by Doura Excelsior, one of the most successful brood mares in history.

During the mid-1990s, the Jerry Wismer family of Amherstburg, Ontario proved worthy with Grand Champion Maplewood Levi bred by Richard Wegner. Other top breeders included Bill and Sharon Dean from Michigan, and David and Wilma Cleghorn who showed full sisters, Thistle Ridge Argyll Beth and "Fancy." In 1996 and 1997, Solomon's Paulette owned by Brad Remus of Osborne, Kansas and bred by Max Remus, was Reserve Grand Champion. Gene and Maureen Emswiler of Hagerstown, Maryland dominated in the Grand Champion Stallion class for three straight years with Live Oak Grandeur by Doura Sensation. His dam was Northumberland Melinda, a champion in 1986.

Live Oak Charming Rhapsody and Live Oak Perfection Charm, owned by the Emswilers, were Champion Mares in 1996 and 1997. Additional outstanding owners and breeders during this time included Andrew and Linda Bentley of Goodrich, Michigan; the Bob Robertson family; Warren and Faye Atwell of Birch Run, Michigan, owners of Zippity Do Dah, a Grand Champion Stallion; and Pat McMahen of 2S Clydesdales, owner of Northumberland Flower Girl. This top mare, a full brother to "Shea" and winner of the "Best of Breed," was bred by Jim Emmons.

In the late 1990s and early 2000s, the leading owners and breeders included the Mike Moleskis; Robert Hamstra of Lynden, Washington, breeder of Mt. Baker's Padro's Ivan by Cedric Padro; Gary and Scott Nebergall of Arthur, Illinois, owners of Green Leaf Prestige by Ayton Perfection; and Dr. Jeff Gower of Springfield, Missouri, owner of Ozark's Royal Double Aristocrat by Caesar of Olde Pine Tree Winston, the Grand Champion Stallion in 2000 and 2001. Others of note were Chuck Cryderman of Richmond, Michigan, and Daryl and Lorraine Cobbs of Huntington, Indiana, owners of Grandview Eli's Just-in-Step, the 2001 Reserve Champion, by Armageddon's Lord Elijah, the Reserve Champion in 1992.

Pinnacle Farms, owned by Thomas Miller of Milan, Illinois, produced the 2001 Grand and Reserve Champion Clydesdale with Barclay's Classic Pearl by Inspector Floss and the imported Hillmoor Anna May. The Six Horse Hitch class was won by Express Clydesdales owned by Bob and Nedra Funk of Yukon, Oklahoma with Donald Langille driving.

Northumberland Flowergirl, Supreme Champion 1998 and 1999 National Shows. She is held by her owner, Pat McMahen, 2S Clydesdales, Houston, Texas. With her are breeder Jim Emmons, Galesville, Wisconsin and his daughter, 1999 National Clydesdale Queen, Kari Brown. Flowergirl is Breyer Horse Model #775.

Outstanding owners and breeders in the early 2000s also included Chester Weber, owner of Live Oak Omega by Ayton Perfection, the 2002 Grand Champion Stallion; the Wismer family, owners of SBH Phoenix by Greendykes Sherman; Ray and Sharon Priebe of Grayling, Michigan; David Carson of Listowel, Ontario, owner of West Plain Chelsea, the Reserve Champion in 2002; and William Burgett of Fredericktown, Ohio, whose Owl Creek Clydesdales won the Six Horse Hitch that year.

Pinnacle Farms shown bright once again in 2003 with the imported Hillmoor Anna May becoming Grand Champion Mare. Other winners were shown by Chuck Cryderman and Bob Robertson of Listowel, Ontario. His Clydesdale Bart, bred by the Horn family of Virden, Manitoba, was Gelding Champion.

In 2004, Don and Kerry Lowes of Princeton, Ontario showed the winner of the Grand Champion Stallion class with Stone Croft Ayton Magic bred by Warren and Maureen Kells of New Hamburg, Ontario. The Grand Champion Mare was Solomon's Asti owned by Chuck Cryderman and Bob Robertson. Reserve Grand Champion Mare honors were garnered by Great American Clydesdales, owned by Jack and Sue Shaw of Orland, Indiana with their Clydesale Grandview Eli's Intrigue by Armageddon Lord Elijah, bred by the Cobbs family. Winner of the Six Horse Hitch competition was Stan White of White Rock Farms, Argyle, Texas.

At the 2005 National Clydesdale Sale in Springfield, Illinois, record crowds, record entries, and record sales were the call of the day. Auctioneers Leroy Yoder and Steve Andrews of Wooster, Ohio whipped potential buyers and enthusiastic onlookers into a frenzy with his folksy and convincing style. The result in all classes was multiple bids like none seen before.

In the Gelding class, Birky's Pride Turbo, a bay with four white legs and a white blaze face consigned by Robert and Andrea Detweiler, Oelwein, Iowa, sold for an astounding $26,000. Proving that investing in Clydesdales can be profitable, this horse could have been purchased for $6,000 the previous fall.

Lisa Banga and Leroy Yoder at 2005 National Sale

Birky's Pride Turbo, top-selling gelding at 2005

In the Mare Class, bidding was furious before Trieste's Betty Grable, a bay with four white legs and a white strip on her face consigned by Chad Cole and Michael Wian, Bellefonte, Pennsylvania, was purchased for $35,000. Her heritage included Bardrill Ambassador and Olde Pine Tree Donegal.

Through the years, Clydesdale ownership has truly been a family matter, with many having loved the breed for generation after generation. These include the Jones family from Wisconsin, the Castagnasso family located in various states, the Polinder family from the state of Washington, the Thurston's from Ogden, Utah, the Clauson/Thoms family from Iowa, the Emmons from Wisconsin, the Wilhoits of Botavia, Iowa, the Browns of Indiana, and Nathan Goff from West Virginia.

In the late 1950s, the Jim and Betty Groves family from Illinois began raising Clydesdales after they rented from a gritty old farmer named Floyd Conger. He worked four of them in his fields. Fascinated with the breed, the Groves began helping Floyd, and when he died they continued his tradition by purchasing the farm and two mares to add to the mix. The name they chose—Glen-Coe, included the "G" from Groves and the "C" from Conger, with the name plucked from a Scottish map sent to them by Maury Telleen. It only took them five years to agree on the choice!

Wismer Family, Jerry, Ron, and Barbara

Jim and Betty Groves

Symbolic of the modern day Clydesdale owners, ones who have carried on the tradition of those who began the breed in North America, is the Jerry and Barbara Wismer family of Amherstburg, Ontario, twenty minutes south of Windsor.

While some have been more financially blessed to compete in the various shows across the continent, Jerry, Barbara, and sons Ronnie, a professional firefighter, and Rick, a moldmaker, are representative of a family that have been able to sustain due to their savvy with the breed. In many ways, the Wismer's parallel a major league baseball team like the Minnesota Twins in their quest to compete with the cash-rich New York Yankees. "We just keep with our strategy, and it works," says Ron.

"At age four or five," Jerry recalls, "I used to get up at daylight and go find my grandfather who had horses pulling a disc or harrow. Then I had a pony, then a better pony, then a riding horse that I rode to town to see Barbara who I had met in the sixth grade. Then I liked quarter horses, but we sold them and I didn't have any horses for ten years. When I was ready, I told my wife I wanted to sit on the wagon and hear the chains rattle and so we decided on draft horses."

First introduced to the Clydesdales by a friend named Bill Taylor who told Jerry, "If you are going to buy a draft horse, buy a Clydesdale," the Wismers' philosophy is to buy and breed, then sell, and breed some more, all the while looking for the champions that will build the reputation of their farm. "This is the formula that we use—buy quality instead of getting into numbers, and then stick with the plan even when times are tough." Jerry, whose grandfather disdained the tractor and insisted on farm animals to work the land, says, "And it can be successful for anyone who is serious about it and tries hard to better himself.

Case in point are two Wismer National Champions, Maplewood Levi (1994) and SBH Phoenix (2003). Levi, PTS Noblemans Danielle, and Faydar Nanette were the featured horses at Carson's Summer Invitational Sale in 1999. It was after this sale that they purchased Phoenix and West Pleans Cassandra, an imported yearling filly from Scotland. Two results—SBH Phoenix, the 2004 Overall Grand Champion at The Royal for the third time and Cedarlane Jewel, the winner at the same prestigious show in the Yearling Filly class, Reserve Junior Champion, Best Ontario

Bred and Sired Yearling Filly and Best Mare any age bred, born, and raised in Canada. This followed her win as Champion Foal in 2003.

"Horses buy horses and even though I love the thrill of raising a champion, at some point it may be time to say goodbye," Ronnie Wismer says. "And since we keep a foal, we still have a part of the horse that we had to sell." Dad Jerry adds, "You want to make the offspring better than their parents. That's why it is so important to study pedigrees."

Top breeders like the Wismers research pedigrees to show the origin of any Clydesdale. "We focus in on horses that we know have good lineage," Jerry Wismer says. "Ones where we have researched at least three generations."

SBH Phoenix, a bay, according to his certificate of registration, "with white blaze face with black spot on muzzle and in left nostril, white splash on left under belly and left girth, legs white to knees and hocks," was bred of Greendykes Sherman and Emerald's Lucky Lady with their heritage including such Clydesdales as Ayton Perfection, Eskechraggan Blossom, Grainyford Kate, Pouton Louise, Northumberland Joy, and Brookside Rose.

"I saw some of the offspring of Ayton Perfection when I was in Scotland," Jerry Wismer recalls, "and I liked them. I then bought a daughter of his named Highland Grace that we showed with great success. I saw Greendykes Sherman as a yearling and watched him over the years as he progressed. I saw Emerald's Lucky Lady when Ray and Sharon Priebe brought her out to show at the Michigan State Fair and I liked her also.

SBH Phoenix's siblings also entered into the Wismers' decision-making process. "I looked at Phoenix's full sister SBH Enchantress and his full brother Limited Edition," Jerry recalled. "I knew these were very good horses and that Phoenix stood to be every bit as good or better. We had our choice of Phoenix or Limited Edition and chose to go with the younger horse. Good families on both sides—that was the key."

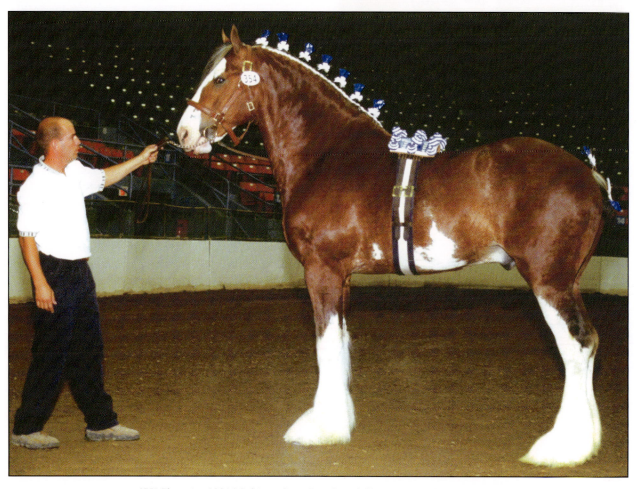

SBH Phoenix, 2001 Michigan State Fair Grand Champion and Ron Wismer

In Cedarlane Jewel's case, the lineage showed that her sire SBH Phoenix was born of Greendykes Sherman [GB] and Emerald's Lucky Lady [USA]. Greendykes Sherman, in turn, was a product of Millisle Perfection [GB] and Grainyford Kate [GB], while Emerald's Lucky Lady was bred of Olde Pine Tree Winston [USA] and Brookside Margie [USA].

Ron Wismer showing Maplewood Levi Grand Champion Stallion at the 1994 National Show

Cedarlane Jewel's dam West Plean Cassandra's lineage traces to parents Greendykes Apollo [GB] and Woodhouse Classic Lady [GB]. Greendykes Appollo was the result of mating Greendykes Chancer [GB] and Welbury Diana [GB], while Woodhouse Classic Lady came from Woodhouse Turbo [GB] and West Forth Maradonna [GB]. "Cassandra was entered in the World Clydesdales Show Sale and we were interested in a filly," Jerry Wismer says. "I discussed her with some of my Scottish friends and learned that she came from a tremendous mother, a big mare who produced some real quality foals. Her action and presence made us think she would be a good hitch mare, which she has turned out to be. Breeding her to Phoenix was a natural since we felt Phoenix had great sire potential. We hoped we could get some foals that could halter as well as hitch and Cedarlane Jewel is off to a great start."

Pitching in is a key element to the success of families like the Wismers, who own no more than fifteen horses or so at a time

West Plean Cassandra, 1st place registered mare cart at 2003 and 2004 National Show, with Ron Wismer driving

compared with large breeders that own many more. "It builds a bond with us," Barbara, who with her husband and sons cleans the stalls, braids the horses, whitens the horse's feather with sawdust, and brightens their coats, emphasizes. "When we work, we work, when we play, we play, but we do it together. The Clydesdales are part of our family and we love them so."

Camaraderie between owners is something that impressed Ronnie Wismer, who relished the competition while he was growing up. "They say that if a horse owner is lost or needs help in some way," he offers, "and has a copy of The Draft Horse Journal, all they have to do is call anyone listed in there and immediately help is on the way. That's the way it is — the closeness of the owners is amazing."

A similar "mom and pop" Clydesdale breeder is located in Bronson, Michigan where Mike and Cheri Moleski own Armageddon Farms. Their story began in the mid-1980s when Cheri fell in love with a black Clydesdale at a county fair in Centerville, Michigan. Soon there were two black Clydesdales roaming their pastures, a rarity since that color represented only about ten percent of the total breed. Through the years, the Moleskis became top breeders with their most outstanding champion a mare named Armageddon Mistress Eve.

Moleski enjoys the camaraderie among the Clydesdale owners, especially those like the Wismers who "own Clydesdales because they simply love the breed." He says he enjoys winning at shows like anyone else, but hopes that the competition doesn't end up being like it is in Scotland, "where those 200 year-old rivalries spoil the fun of owning a Clydesdale."

Top Clydesdale breeder Darryl Cobbs of Grandview Farms in Indiana raised quarter horses before becoming enchanted with Clydesdales. First up was Danny, a former Anheuser Busch horse. "We went to fairs, and watched the various draft horses," Darryl recalls. "But the Clydes were classier, they had the beautiful feather, the good attitude, they were truly gentle giants."

Cobbs, whose family operation includes wife Lorraine, son Shannon, and daughter-in-law Justine, said Danny was followed by Duffy, and then Elizabeth. She's an "'Ever Ready Battery' type of mare who is still giving us babies today."

The Clydesdale's ability to perform on cue has always impressed Cobbs, whose hitch team won overall honors at the 2004 Springfield, Massachusetts show. "Hitch horses are more spirited," he says. "In the stall, they can be like teddy bears, but when it's show time, they turn Hollywood. Only a few horses out there will show off like that."

Justine Cobbs at the Britt, Iowa Draft Horse Show

Tucker and Katie resting before their ride in the parade.

Bryce and Jake Derrer discussing issues with Jack the Clydesdale

Another outstanding Clydesdale family operation is overseen by owner Steve Gregg, with wife Beth, of Gregglea Clydesdales of Cargill, Ontario. Winners with Erin and Ginger (three-year-old mares) of the Two Horse Team category at the 2004 Toronto show, Steve is a fourth generation breeder whose grandfather George began raising Clydesdales in 1926. Like the Wismers, Steve, and his dad Alan before him, believe in "raising them, selling them, and then taking satisfaction in watching others do well with them. This is what surprises owners of other breeds, that we are a family of breeders who want to help others as much as possible."

The Gregg Family, (R to L)
Steve, Beth, Jason and Janine

For his family, raising Clydesdales has been a blessing. "We have no hired help," says Steve, who along with Beth introduced the Clydesdales to Hawaii when the Westin Resort decided to own a team. "It's all within our family. Kids, nephews—all of us working together."

Historian, breeder, and competition judge Jim Emmons fell in love with Clydesdales because his father, V. Raymond Emmons, was in love with them when Jim was four years old. As early as 1915, the family had owned Percherons, but the first Clydes, Senator's Belle and Senator's Mabel, were purchased from August Busch, Jr.

"Dad was a neighbor to Eben and Floyd Jones," Jim recalls. "He raised Clydesdales, and soon that was what dad was doing. And through the years, my parents, my two brothers, a sister, my daughter, a nephew, a cousin, and I have kept the family tradition going."

This tradition, like that of the Wismers', the Moleskis', the Cobbs', and the Greggs', is an essential building block for the longevity of the breed. Generation after generation continues to keep the flame burning and a love for the Clydesdales at the center of their commitment. "It's all about the horse, everything for the Clydesdales," Jerry Wismer says. "Hopefully they will continue to be bred for a thousand years after I am gone."

Andale Empress with Jim Emmons at the lead proves that not all Clydesdales have four white legs. Reserve champion at the 1992 and 1995 national shows, she was bred and owned by Roger and Virginia Emmons, Bangor, Wisconsin.

Longtime Clydesdale Breeders of the U.S.A. board member Lisa Banga of Watseka, Illinois shares Wismer's passion for the community of Clydesdale owners. "I was raised with Percherons," she says, "but in the mid-1980s I gained a new family when I began to love the Clydesdale. My friend Bill Muir from Scotland and others showed me the wonder of the animal and how everyone helps everyone out. To my amazement, I saw that owners teach other owners and breeders their tricks, ones that permit them to beat each other in competition. How refreshing this was. When you have a member of the Clydesdale family as a friend, there is nothing they wouldn't do for you."

New Clydesdale owners pop up every day as horse lovers decide the breed is something they want to pursue. Each year more than six hundred new Clydesdales are registered, continuing the tradition of Clydesdale ownership with families such as the Wismers, the Greggs, the Cobbs, the Moleskis, Jack and Sue Shaw, and the Edwin Henkens of Washington state.

To honor those that have contributed to the welfare and promotion of the Clydesdales, the Clydesdale Breeders of the U.S.A. established the Heritage Hall of Fame. Among the recipients of the award have been Colonel Robert Holloway, the Jones family, August A. Busch, Jr., Chester Weston, Berry Farrell, Paul Cooper, Don Castagnasso, and Fred Polinder, with many more to come.

To be certain, the resurrection of the breed through the Milwaukee Circus Parade, *The Draft Horse Journal*, and the efforts of August Busch, Jr., and the Budweiser Clydesdales is being carried on by family after family of breeders and Clydesdale lovers around the globe. Popularity with the breed is a given, for they are a slice of history—a recollection of a simpler time when the world was not consumed with a fast-food mentality but instead a quest to keep things simple. Clydesdales, with their combination of strength and calm, of loyalty and steadiness, provide a reminder that recalling the past and learning from it is something to be cherished.

Luis Brooks snuggles up to his favorite two Clydesdales

"Men are generally more careful of the breeding of their horses and dogs than of their children."

— William Penn,
*Some Fruits of Solitude,
in Reflections and Maxims
Relating To The Conduct
of Human Life.*

Owning A Clydesdale

Young Sierra Brooke Covell kisses her Clydesdale. Sierra is still involved with Clydesdales

Shania, a mare stands watch with Miles, a foal, owned by Jeanne Williams, Woodside, California

Why own a Clydesdale? Easy question, easy answers.

Clydesdales make wonderful companions.
They bond the family.
They respect other horses and humans alike.
They have a calm demeanor we can emulate.
They are gentle, never feisty or argumentative.
They have a consistent temperament.
They are givers, not takers.
They don't mind working and take direction easily.
They are smart and behave with manners.
Kids develop good work habits taking care of them.
Youngsters can learn about handling birth and death from them.
They won't step on you with their big feet (unless you are in the wrong place).
They know how to share.
Lessons about buying and selling animals can be learned.
They are competitive, but not aggressive.
They love the simple pleasure of grazing in the pasture.
They are gentle with youngsters.
You can ride them safely.
You can watch them sleeping standing up.
They have a quiet confidence about them.
They recognize sounds and commands you can teach them.
They are excellent Moms and Dads.
They represent strength.
They live to a ripe old age.
You can dress them up on the Fourth of July and fireworks don't scare them.
They are part of a colorful history and folklore.
Naming them is fun for you and your kids.
They don't eat as much as people think they do.

Rex Mann of 2S Clydesdales, winner of Sr. Showmanship at the National Clydesdale show

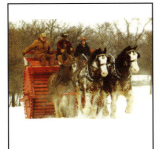

David Stalheim drives four Clydesdales pulling a snow roller.

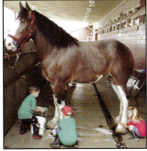

Wismer grandchildren

Rebecca Cannon of Cleveland, Tennessee

If a person is convinced that owning a Clydesdale makes good "horse sense," and why wouldn't it, then what's next? The key to ownership is education about the breed— what kinds of Clydesdales are there? What "horse" age makes sense? What are the characteristics of a good one? How much do they cost? Where can they be purchased? And, most important, what is the proper way to care for them?

One terrific source of information is the Clydesdales Education Foundation, the nonprofit organization dedicated to providing cultural, historical, and educational information about the breed. More about this organization can be learned at www.ClydesUSA.com.

If the Clydesdale is simply going to be a pet, then he or she is going to be chosen like one would choose a dog or cat. There are no worries about pedigree and such, just a gentle giant that can roam the pasture and look good at photo op time. Many Clydesdale owners choose their horses simply by the way they look, their names, or how they cuddle up to the prospective owner when they meet.

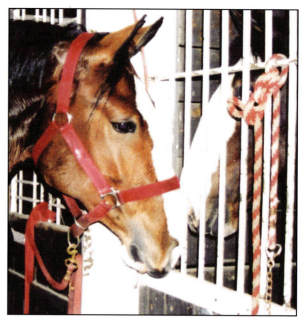

Horses sniffing

A Clydesdale will carry on a conversation, albeit in his or her own special way. An owner may hear a mare wicker softly to a foal and hear the same sound when it's close to breakfast or dinnertime. If a whinny, a grunt or a squeal is heard, the horse is probably excited. A snort means they may be upset or feel they are in danger.

Three Clydesdales in a row

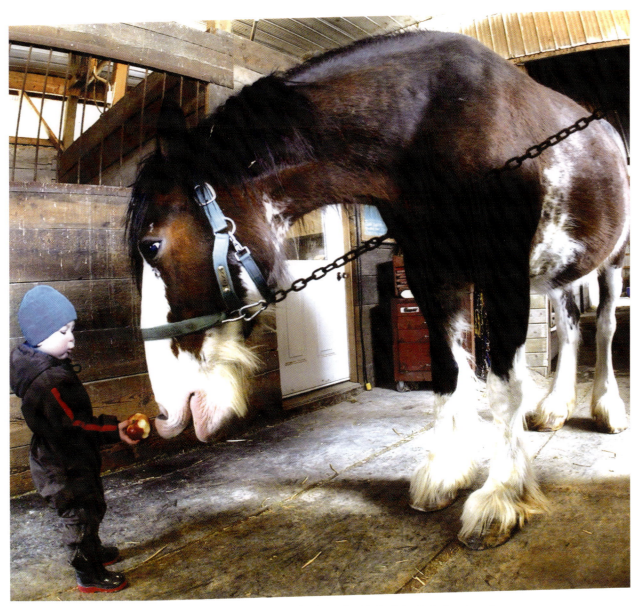
Nicholas Wismer feeding apple to his friendly Clydesdale, Cedarlane Jasmine

The tone of the owner's voice is more important than the words spoken when attempting to comfort or reassure a Clydesdale. If the horse actually speaks, call a psychiatrist.

A Clydesdale's ears (watch them as they rotate to the area of interest) are antennae of information about their state of mind. If they are pricked forward, the horse has an interest in an apple or other goody being held or another horse or human walking by. If the ears are tilted backwards, the horse is curious about something behind them. Laid back ears signal displeasure, temper, or perhaps an aggressive attitude. Relaxed ears mean the horse is happy as can be.

If a tail begins to swish, the horse is either swatting at flies or is irritated. Like a dog that is happily panting away, tongue extended, a horse that is content lets its head hang down with bottom lip relaxed and tongue extended and eyes partially closed indicating that it is at peace with the world.

In the pasture, notice that just as with humans, there is a distinctive pecking order with Clydesdales. The more aggressive ones will assert domination, the meeker take a back seat.

Clydesdales love to be petted. They also enjoy a snack whether it is apples, carrots, donuts, or chewy caramels. They are picky. When offered a snack for the first time, they will usually take their time before deciding whether to chomp on it. Many times when a donut is given to them for the first time in a bucket of grain, they will eat around the donut until the pail is empty except for the donut. Then they will sniff, and sniff some more until they either eat the donut or decide to leave it alone. The same thing occurs with medicine mixed in with food.

Those selecting Clydesdales with intention to show, but not breed, are another class of owners. Paying attention to the tips provided in the next chapter regarding what judges look for when they are deciding the winners and losers in competition is crucial. Using these criteria, a Clydesdale can be chosen that possesses the suggested characteristics. A consultant may be employed to assist

Great American Clydesdales delivering Christmas turkeys in Orland, Indiana

any purchase, someone savvy in the nuances of what makes a Clydesdale good for show purposes. Helpful publications include two by Marion Young: *A Beginner's Guide to Basic Conformation and Judging of Clydesdales* and *A Beginners Guide to Basic Show Preparation and Showmanship of Clydesdales.*

If one intends to become a breeder of Clydesdales, it is important to select horses that will reproduce in accordance with the selected game plan. Many different systems of breeding exist dependent on the size of the pocketbook and how large a herd of horses is desired. A trip to Grant's Farm, the Budweiser operation in St. Louis, may be quite advisable to see firsthand how the organization operates its successful breeding program.

Nicholas Wismer feeding straw to his Clydesdale pal, Cedarlane Skipper

Breeding is tricky business for the uninitiated, and working with experienced Clydesdale owners is advised. Only about half of the mares bred each year conceive and sometimes the foals don't survive, a heartbreaking experience for the owner. Clydesdales are a bit brittle as well, with permanent injury an unfortunate certainty for many.

Charles Cryderman, owner of Greenwood Farms in Richmond, Michigan, suggests to those interested in Clydesdales that they "work with credible people." He adds, "Go to shows and walk around. You can tell who knows what they are doing and who doesn't. And ask around—people in the Clydesdale world are the friendliest you will ever find. Everyone helps everyone else despite the competition."

Cryderman emphasizes, "Quality over quantity . . . Think about using a consultant," he says. "And buy the best mare or stallion you can find based on your finances. Then build from there."

"There is no perfect Clydesdale," Jim Emmons says. "There is a hole in every horse. But that doesn't mean you can't find

Where can I buy a Clydesdale?

Each April, the Clydesdale Breeders of the U.S.A. holds its Annual Meeting and conducts the National Clydesdales Sale in Springfield, IL. This sale is the largest offering of purebred Clydesdales horses in the world with about 180-200 head of Clydesdale horses being cataloged each year. Educational seminars are also held at this event.

the most important characteristics. In a stallion, you want a big drafty horse. Bigger than the mares, big-footed, plenty of hair, and heavy bone structure. So get a big stallion, and then the mare can be more feminine, not as big, with neater, finer hair."

"Specific size," Emmons says, "depends on the point of view and strategy, but seventeen-one, seventeen-two (hands) is good for the mare, with eighteen or eighteen-one for the stallion." To estimate how tall a young horse will be at maturity can be learned, according to Jerry Wismer, by dropping a string from the elbow to the bottom of the ankle and then swinging it upward to the wither. "Works every time," Wismer says.

"No matter, you have to be patient to see how Clydesdales will turn out," says Wismer, who, like his fellow owners, is a gambler of sorts. "It will take five, six years to see whether you have a champion. Sometimes longer."

Breeder Mike Moleski believes "farm visits" are important for those considering Clydesdale ownership. "I'm not a fan of attending sales and buying the horse there," he says. "I like to see them at their farm, check their lineage, know if they are being cared for with a 'hands-on' attitude. I especially want to know about the mare since, to my way of thinking, she is 75% of the equation with the stallion being 25%."

The Anheuser Busch experts suggest that selected stallions be three or four years old. Checking lineage is critical and easy to do based on accurate records kept for each horse. If a person is new to breeding, con-

Tracey Robertson exhibiting for Greenwood Farms, Richmond, Michigan

Dr. Chuck Hansell and his wife Ginger drive their 16-year-old registered roan Clydesdale gelding Ben at the Columbus Carriage Days, Wisconsin

sultants can assist as well as those in the Clydesdale business that are pleased to provide any advice required.

Broodmares, according to the Budweiser breeders, should be three years old before breeding the first time. Any prospective breeder wants to pay close attention to size, coloring, conformation, foot quality, soundness, and, also of importance, disposition. The mare's fertile period is every twenty-one days during the breeding season.

Whether the foal is born in the serenity of a green pasture or a clean stall makes no difference. Grass or straw will provide the bassinette, and the 125 to 150-pound beauty will be licked nearly to death by mom shortly after birth. All the while, the mother carries on like an automobile inspector checking each vital part of her little one beginning with the ears.

Nature's way of protecting the mare's uterus from being damaged by the foal while in the womb involves the softening of its hooves. Within twenty-four to seventy-two hours after birth, the hooves begin to harden.

Watching a newborn foal attempt to stand up for the first time is exciting. Within the first half hour or so after birth, he or she is very clumsy and this will not improve until three hours or so after foaling. Nursing will usually occur quickly and once again nature protects the tiny creature through the mother's milk that contains an overabundance of proper vitamins and antibodies to provide the foal with a protective system.

The first three months of a foal's life is critical to survival, and thus constant care is advised. More information about the entire foaling experience is available through a brochure titled *Clydesdales Foaling Tips*, a publication of the Clydesdale Breeders of the U.S.A.

Clydesdales may be first shown in competition while they are weanlings, less than a

First meeting of mare and foal. Green Leaf Raine nuzzles her first foal, Sioux Creek's Raine Beaux. Owned by Linda Sioux Stenson of Loveland, Colorado. Linda rides Raine for recreation, drives her at combined driving events, and shows her in halter.

year old. Then they move up to the yearling classes, then the two-year-old classes. At this point, they are about half-grown, with full maturity not occurring until they are about five years old.

Today, a person wishing to become a Clydesdale owner can purchase a horse for as little as a thousand dollars. Some sell for much more—as much as $40,000. Attending horse shows and auctions is the best way to see the wide variety of Clydesdale horses available, but every novice is advised to do their homework and talk to seasoned Clydesdales owners, judges, and consultants who can offer valuable advice before making their first purchase.

Caring for Clydesdales is a labor of love. A typical day begins with their opening their eyes around sunrise after a good night's rest. If they have been covered through the night, the blanket is removed as they enjoy a fresh bucket of water drawn from a nearby spigot.

An adult Clydesdale will drink a minimum of 10-12 gallons in the course of the day, usually more. After a few large gulps, it's breakfast time, with the menu featuring alternative main courses including mixtures of oats and other grains with perhaps some molasses and salt thrown in for good measure. A bit of hot water may soup up the feed a bit.

How much grain? For the average Clydesdale, this would be between two to five pounds, placed in a trough positioned just high enough so they can bend their head and eat heartily. Slowly, the tasty treat is swooped into the horse's large jaw as slivers fall to the barn floor. The water should be close by so that a drink can help the horse digest the dry food.

Once the main course has been served, fifteen to twenty pounds of grass hay is dumped into a hay bin to provide for snacks throughout the day. A salt lick, necessary since the horse needs large amounts of salt, is suggested in every stall.

If the rumble of a Clydesdale is heard toward sunset, it means they are hungry again. Lunch is not required, but dinner is essential to providing the necessary nourishment the horse desires. Duplication of the

Famous Reggie White - Best American Bred Gelding. Exhibited by Cal and Judy Larson, Ripon, Wisconsin

Thistle Ridge Royal Merrilee, 1st place Sr. Filly foal and Best Foal at the 2004 National Show. Exhibited by Karl and Jan Stewart, Beeton, Ontario, Canada

morning meal is usual, with the owner keeping tabs on weight control (if necessary) so that the Clydesdale doesn't end up outgrowing his stall.

Clydesdales possess a very slow digestive system and it is thus necessary to provide exercise time when they finish eating. Directing them to the nearest pasture does the trick so they can stretch, graze, and perhaps roam with their Clydesdale buddies.

At some point in the day, it may be time for hair and make-up. Proper grooming is essential not only to the look of the animal, but to keep them clean so that deadly diseases can be prevented. Just like humans, the Clydesdale enjoys a good bath and the swipe of the soft currycomb and other brushes are used to keep every hair in place both up top and with the feather toward the bottom. Because of the heavy hair feather, skin care is a must since Clydesdales are susceptible to skin problems that can cause them irritation.

The list of "make-up" tools can be endless, but the basics include a dandy brush that is used to remove dust and dirt from the skin, a sweat scraper to remove any excess moisture, a body brush to brush the horse's body, a grooming cloth to polish the coat and keep it shiny, a hoof pick to dislodge mud, manure, and stones from the bottom of the horse's feet, a rubber or metal currycomb to remove any scurf in the hair, and yes, a horse vacuum cleaner to sweep up any excess dirt and to fluff up the hair. Most Clydesdales just stand and enjoy the one-half to three-quarters of an hour experience imagining perhaps that they are simply being cared for at what might be called a horse spa. This is because the effects of currycombing are akin to a masseuse since there is a gentle, sweeping stroke applied to the neck, withers, shoulders, backside, belly, and hind legs. Compared to currycombing, brushing the horse is a stronger application that is applied to the mane and tail.

A clean Clydesdale is a happy Clydesdale

Sawdusting a Clydesdale's feather makes it shiny and white

Any collection of film that may have accumulated on the horse's mane is swept away with a cleansing agent called castile soap. Using regular soap would sap the body of valuable oils and cause dry skin. A good rinse like those at a car wash completes the washing process.

A day at the barbershop includes trimming the hair of the ears, by the jaw, and under the neck. The mane is pulled from time to time, but never the feather, even when they envelope the hooves and touch the ground. By walking, the horse will be its own feather barber. Castile soap is used to keep them white and shiny, with the process taking a half hour or so of lathering. Once they have been cleaned, a hose supplies the necessary rinse after which clean, fine sawdust is applied for drying purposes.

Before a show, owners use talcum powder to whiten the feather. Sometimes the Clydesdales enter the show ring in a cloud of white powder, as if from a dream sequence. A tip for the novice Clydesdale owner or fan is to never say "feathers" but "feather."

Braiding the tail and rolling the mane are also essential elements to the Clydesdale's grooming process. The latter enhances the horse's luster, while the former provides a more statuesque portrayal of the horse's hips and also prevents the tail from swishing to and fro against the other horses if they are pulling a wagon.

Braiding the tail is a fine art, one learned from experience. Three clean untangled strands are woven together. A ribbon is then used to provide the human necktie effect. Strands of string work as the glue to keep the hairy ball together.

Rolling the mane requires patience and strength. Two forty-inch lengths of ribbon bunting are the key as the strands of hair are twisted together. A slipknot holding the lumped braid keeps everything in order.

If need be, the three and three-quarters pound horseshoes are removed and reset, usually on a four to six week basis. This appears as if it might hurt the horse, but it doesn't. Even the removing of the handcrafted shoes with a proper tool doesn't inflict any pain since the horse came equipped with pads that blunt the force being used. Watching this process is fascinating as the ferrier slides a hand down the horse's leg until reaching the fetlock. He or she then straddles the Clydesdale's leg with their own while holding the selected hoof in their hands. With the proper tool (pull offs), eight number twelve three-inch long nails in the horseshoe are removed until the dinner-plate-sized shoe, one costing somewhere in the neighborhood of $30, clanks on the barn floor. All the while, the Clydesdale stands gently composed as if nothing is occurring out of the ordinary.

While all of the elements of good grooming are important, the Clydesdale is a horse that loves to be loved. Talking to horses too much on a regular basis might be cause for concern, but chatting with them is something they enjoy especially when entering their stall or approaching them from behind. Startling a Clydesdale is not easy due to their superior smell and ability to see behind them, but sneaking up on one is not a good idea.

Reading Clydesdales and their mood is an art learned through experience. Veteran trainer and driver Richard Derrer says, "Horses can be nervous if they know you are nervous. When you know they may feel

Ryma Brooks putting bright flowers in a Clydesdale's mane

threatened, don't look them directly in the eye but instead focus on their shoulders. With many of them it's 'fight or flight,' and you want to ease up to them, give them some comfort so they don't feel like you are forcing them. And give them plenty of room so they don't think they are being crowded."

Derrer also stresses being positive with the horses, especially at the end of the day or the end of a training period. "Horses remember real well," he says, "and you want them to take something positive to the stall with them. Even if you are having trouble getting them to back up, help them take one step backwards and then quit. They will remember that the next day when the training resumes. Praise them, they like that."

Clydesdales owners and breeders treat their animals like one of the family and take care of them in a like manner. They may be giant-sized, but they have the heart and soul of a child, and give back a thousandfold the love given to them.

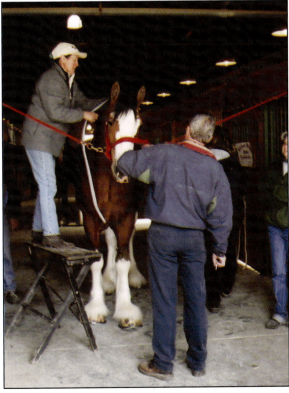

Rolling a Clydesdale's mane takes practice and skill

The World's Most Magical Horse

Courtney Mac Gillirary of Saddle Rock Clydesdales, Drury, Missouri peeks out from under the head of Gruffy

"What do you want?" a Clydesdale seems to think

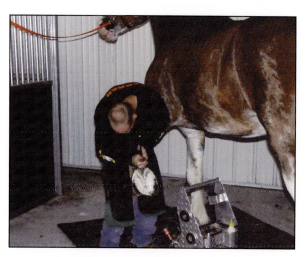

Rusty Derrer Shoeing a Clydesdale

A thirsty Clydesdale takes a sip of cold water

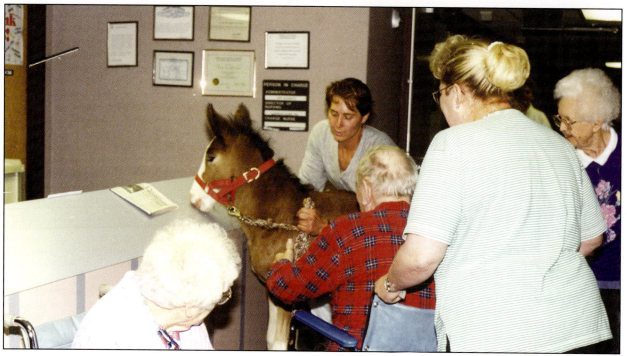

Marsha (five days old) visiting a nursing home to spread joy

Shay Weirick of Augusta, Michigan jumps her Clydesdale over a fence

The World's Most Magical Horse

"Horse sense is the thing a horse has which keeps it from betting on people.."

— W. C. Fields

Showing The Clydesdales – Where and How

Owl Creek Clydesdales owned by Bill Burgett of Fredricktown, Ohio,
2004 National Show 1st place Eight-Horse-Hitch

Great American Clydesdales at Elkhart County 4-H Fair, July 25, 2004
Richard Derrer Driver, Travis Leeman Assistant Driver

There is nothing more elegant than Clydesdales performing in a show ring. With pride, they simply mesmerize the crowd with their majestic manner, their high-stepping prance, and a calm similar to the one they portray while quietly grazing in a serene pasture.

Exhibiting Clydesdales is fun and is a chance to bond with "the family" of breeders who share one thing in common—a love for the breed. There are many shows around the country where Clydesdales can be entered in competition. They include the National Clydesdale Show at the Wisconsin State Fair; the Michigan Great Lakes International at Lansing, Michigan; and the Eastern Regional at Harrisburg, Pennsylvania. Others of interest are the Mid-America Clydesdale Show at the Indiana State Fair; the Keystone International Livestock Expo at Harrisburg, Pennsylvania; the Western Regional Show at Monroe, Washington; the Rocky Mountain Regional at Ogden, Utah; the Michigan, Minnesota, Ohio, Illinois, and Iowa State Fairs; and the National Clydesdale Show held each year in Springfield, Illinois. Similar events occur at the Draft Horse Classic and the Los Angeles County Fair in California, the National Western Stock Show in Denver, and the Georgia National Fair. Many local county fairs also hold draft horse shows. They are a good place to learn everything about the breed.

The Clydesdale Breeders Association of the U.S.A. posts a yearly schedule. It can be referenced at either www.Clydesusa.com or by calling 815.247.8780.

Besides numerous shows in England and Scotland, an international show of renown is The Royal Agricultural Winter Fair held in November in Toronto. Created in 1922 by William Dryden, a highly respected breeder of sheep and Shorthorn cattle and the owner of Maple Shade, a family farm just north of present day Oshawa, the program not only

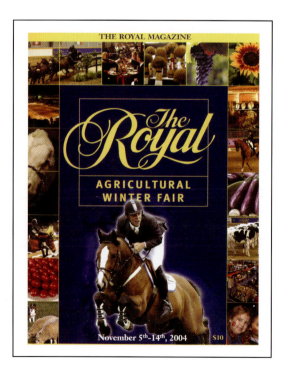

Royal Agricultural Winter Fair Program Cover

Brookside Clydesdales 4 Horse Hitch, Merle Brooks and his Daughter Faith at the 2004 Scott County Fair, Jordan Minnesota

features a revered horse show but something for everyone in the family. One Sunday's program included a cooking school, a cow-milking demonstration, a seminar called "All About Chickens" and another labeled "Celebration of the Dog," as well as the Canadian National Aberdeen Angus Show and a spectacular horse show in the main ring. One highlight is young riders jumping their ponies in competition.

Another feature is the Clydesdale Halter Judging Competition, staged near the barn where the exhibitors display their colors and welcome visitors in awe of the large animals. A sort of "tailgate party" atmosphere prevails at these shows, with kids and adults alike presented with an up-close and personal look at the famous breed and owners willing to go out of their way to answer questions about each horse and its breeding. Petting is the order of the day since the Clydesdales love the people who love them.

Once the decision is made to show a Clydesdale, it is important to understand the alternative classes available. Stallions, mares, and geldings may be shown, in age groups ranging from weanlings to aged horses. Guidelines, deadlines, and rules can be obtained from the breeder's association.

An exciting part of any show is the filly competition. Normally divided into classes based on age, the youngsters are led into the ring with all the fervor of a baby just beginning to explore the world. Many owners leave the horse's hair long and soap it to provide a wooly teddy bear appearance. In November, the horses are already growing their long winter hair.

Watching the various halter classes compete is dramatic as the judges attempt to decide which horses are superior. The team and hitch competitions provide a panoramic spectacle with the high-steppers wearing the harness and pulling the wagon. Seeing the Clydesdales in all of their green, red, yellow, white, and deep blue regalia, akin to the colors worn by thoroughbreds under jockey silks, is something never to be forgotten, especially for kids that see the giants as something out of a fairy tale book.

In the hitch class, the competitors attempt to outshine their fellow "teamsters" in classes such as the Clydesdale 2 Wheel Cart for mares and geldings, the Clydesdale 3 Horse Team Unicorn Hitch, and the Clydesdale 4, 6, and 8 Horse Hitch. Prize money is earned in addition to the ribbons designating a championship performance.

Choosing hitch horses takes special care according to Ned Niemiec of Hallamore Clydesdales, Lakeville, Massachusetts. "With the lead horse, you want a horse that carries itself well," he says. "It needs to move well, be sort of a peacock-type horse whereas the wheel horses will be rugged, solid horses."

Hitch driving is a special talent," says Niemiec, a driver for twenty-six years. "Drivers need a good strong set of hands and steady nerves with no panic. Drivers have to have confidence, sort of a self-assured posture."

Hallamore's magnificent eight-horse Clydesdale hitch driven by Ned Niemiec has become a traditional attraction at many New England fairs, parades, and special events

David Stalhiem drives his pair of Clydesdale geldings, Bullet and Striker, at the 2003 National Clydesdale Show

Clydesdale owners have multiple reasons for showing their horses in competition. Some do so to promote their breeding prowess, some because they want to continue a family tradition. Others show Clydesdales because they love the competition and realize that winning boosts the prices of their horses at selling-time. Many love the family atmosphere of the various shows, believing that their children learn valuable lessons by becoming involved in the presentation of the horses in alternate classes. Most love the "characters" one meets at competitions, for the Clydesdale lover is a different breed from those who love thoroughbreds and racing horses.

How to show Clydesdales is an art form that stems from knowledge and experience. For novices, the first thing to consider is a thorough knowledge of the "regions of the breed." Terms like "feather" (willowy hair above the hooves), "withers" (the ridge between the shoulder bones of a horse), and "hock" (comparable to the human knee, but elevated and on the hind leg), will be common knowledge.

Attendance at shows like the ones mentioned previously is critical to a continuing education about the breed. While attending, one interested in the breed should do so as a prospective Clydesdale owner who will show horses one day. Sitting in the bleachers and enjoying the competition is fine, but walking around the arena, viewing the horses and their caretakers up close and personal is of great benefit. Visiting the stalls and talking to Clydesdale owners is advisable. They are friendly folks who welcome enthusiasm from a prospective horse owner.

Class being judged at Toronto Royal Agricultural Winter Fair

Live Oak Grandeur, Grand Champion Clydesdale Stallion at 1996 Keystone Invitational

An excellent publication on the showing of Clydesdales and other breeds is called *So You Want To Show Draft Horses*. Published by the staff of the *Draft Horse Journal*, it contains information valuable to any horse owner interested in competition. Included is an excellent article titled "Judging Horses" by Jack Briggs, former superintendent of horses at Cornell University. Realizing what judges look for is paramount to the learning process, and Briggs provides several valuable comments to keep in mind when showing horses, whatever the class may be.

Briggs begins by suggesting that the first rule of thumb, as mentioned above, is to know thoroughly "the important physical characteristics of any domestic animal . . . and have the ability to recognize them." He then points out that, "You must know why they are important [since] if you cannot relate FORM to FUNCTION the whole exercise is meaningless." He adds, "A wide heel and a long sloping pastern are not 'good' because some panel of judges decided that was the case 100 years ago. They are important because they contribute to the usefulness of the animal. And so it is, or should be, with other points of conformation."

To embellish on this statement, Briggs quotes R. B. Ogilvie, a former secretary of the Clydesdales Association. He said, "Utility in a draft horse means absolute soundness, a willingness to work, wearing qualities, and the ability to move large loads at a long, easy stride. Accessories to these desirable qualities in a drafter are oblique shoulders, short backs, deep ribs, long level quarters with heavily muscled thighs extending well down to the hocks, shanks of ample size and quality, pasterns properly set, and strong, shapely feet."

According to Mr. Briggs, the first impression of a horse in competition is every bit as important as it is for a budding romance. "The draft horse," he wrote while providing advice to beginning judges, "is a large animal. That first impression should be gained at a reasonable distance. The general impression will often carry the day, unless [one] finds something they don't like on closer inspection."

Regarding movement of the horse, Briggs stated, "Any horse, light or heavy, is an animal of movement. Whether the purpose of the breed be to draw a load or carry a rider, the feet and legs constitute the working foundation of any horse . . . So I feel that close inspection of a draft horse should begin at the ground, for if he doesn't have it there—he doesn't have what it takes."

Keying in on this last point should cause any prospective owner of Clydesdales that will be showing his horses to concentrate from the bottom up since Briggs obviously feels that when a judge watches a horse trot or walk, back and forth, they will focus on the legs and feet first and the rest of the bulk later.

Every judge has their own manner of deciding what is important to them. Scotland's Shona Zawadzki says she looks for "presence, what first catches my eye, the breed quality,

Pinnacle's Lucky Strike owned by Alan Knobloch, Princeville, Illinois

what fills the eye." Other characteristics important to her include "clean flat bone, not a rounded one, hind legs tall and well-set, good ankles with large feet and silky feather." When the horse is moving, she watches closely whether "the hocks turn inward."

Jim Emmons, a judge in many national events, looks at several features of the horses when walking around them in the show ring. "When they are moving away, I watch closely to see if the hocks are close together," he says. "And the hock action, up and down is important."

Regarding the look of the Clydesdales being judged, Emmons says, "I look to see the shape of the front legs, whether there is

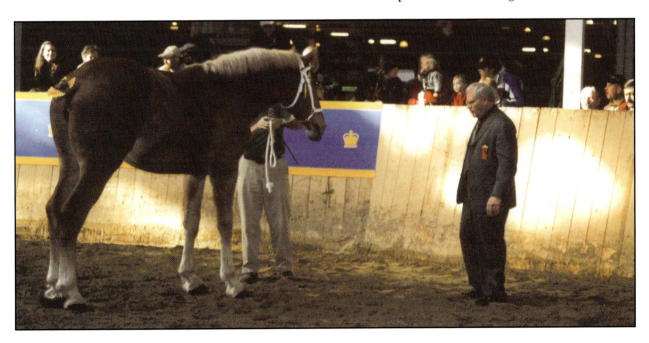

Jim Emmons judging at Toronto Royal Agricultural Winter Fair

Eight-year-old Andy Freitag and five-day-old Northumberland Commander at the 1975 National Show. Commander grew up and was sold to Stuart Anderson, Seattle, Washington.

Andy Freitag grew up and drove the winning Six-Horse-Hitch at the 2000 National Show for Highland Farms, Paris, Kentucky

a square knee, if there is a long pastern at a preferred angle of 45 degrees. The feather should be silky, not thick, and hang straight. A tidy ankle is good with no swelling. Width in the hips is also a plus as is width in the hooves and heels."

Longtime breeder Richard Wegner, as resplendent in the ring as his horses, says he first looks "high" and then "low." After his daughter became interested in a Belgian, Richard decided to enter the heavy horse arena in 1972 with the purchase of a Clydesdale mare named April. His love for the breed continued on at his farm near Clinton, Michigan.

"I first look at the top when deciding on the quality of the horse," Wegner says. "The higher the head on a stallion, the better. There should be no Roman nose, a nice blaze, with the back nice and firm, strong, no sinking down, no swayed back, don't want him to look like someone kicked him in the rear end."

Once the "top" of the horse has been considered, Wagner heads south. "The feet are next," he says. "Someone told me a long time ago that you don't have a good horse unless they have a good bottom. This means the hocks must have good bone structure and the hooves must be wide, properly shaped, no cracks. With the feather, it has to be nice and long, heavy, silky, not course, hanging straight down. Then I look at the amount of light from ground to body, the height of the horse. Mares ought to be about seventeen-two, stallions, eighteen hands or so. Color is more important in the sale ring than in the show ring."

The action of the horse is important to Wegner. "With Solomon's Commodore," Richard says, "he would stand around while we fixed him up and be nonchalant, almost like he was bored. Then right before we went in the ring, I would jiggle his chain, and say 'wake up.' He would come alive, and when he went into the ring and started prancing around with that high-stepping way of his, the quiet crowd began to clap and there was a definite roar. I called him 'the high stepping prince,' and that's the kind of Clydesdale everyone wants to own, one with plenty of action to them."

> ### How long is a pregnancy, and how much do foals weigh?
>
> A typical pregnancy lasts for eleven months. A newborn foal can weigh 110 to 180 lbs. A broodmare (mother to a foal) may produce 100 lbs. of milk daily, and the foal can gain up to four pounds a day for the first few months of life.

Debate continues over how large a champion Clydesdale should be. In Europe, the smaller stature is preferred, but the American Clydesdale, perhaps due to the popularity of the Budweiser team, is preferred of larger stock. Some disagree with this trend, believing that like basketball players, the taller and heavier they are, the more wear and tear on the knees and legs. Judges in America appear to favor the larger Clydesdales though many a champion has been of lighter build.

Most important, experts agree, are the feet and feather. "Watch any good judge and you'll see his nose on the ground," Jim Needham, a Canadian breeder says. "They are checking the feet, the hooves, and the feather."

An excellent publication concerning the basics of horse showing is *Showing Guidelines* published by the Clydesdale Breeders of the U.S.A. The brochure provides information on preparation before a show, what to concentrate on at the show, and specific helpful hints regarding halter exhibition and cart and wheel exhibition. A typical show class listing is an added benefit with as many as 36 separate award classes included.

Clydesdales owners and breeders show their horses with pride. For many, it's the competition, but for others it's simply to provide enjoyment for millions of fans that flock to see the huge horses in all of their color and finery. If Clydesdales could sign autographs, there would be lines around the show ring for they are truly the rock stars of the horse world, proud as can be of their performance capabilities.

David Stalhiem and his daughter Christy at the 2004 Scott County Fair, Jordan, Minnesota

"A horse. A horse. My kingdom for a horse!"

—William Shakespeare,
King Richard III,
Act V, Scene 4

Horse Yarns – Some May Even Be True

Austin Banga and his special Clydesdale

"Get off your high horse!" or "You eat like a horse."

Yes, it's true—these age-old sayings may be attributed to the heavy horse, the Clydesdales in particular. Who first said them is anybody's guess, but first mention dates back to the 1800s in Scotland.

No one, of course, takes credit for, "You're a horse's a___," "It's a horse of a different color," or other remarks involving over three hundred and fifty breeds of horse. How about "Quit horsing around?" Maybe "You can lead a horse to water but you can't make him drink."

Other horse quotes of note that are used everyday include, "High tail it," "Chomping at the bit," "Hold your horses," and "Never look a gift horse in the mouth" (want to know how old a horse is—one can tell by the horse's teeth).

Over the years, the Clydesdale, one of more than 75 million horses in the world, has been the subject of story after story focusing on their intelligence, their friendship, their loyalty, and their grace. Betty Groves recalls her loved one, a horse named King, out on the pasture bordering the county road fronting their farm. As she watched from a distance, she kept expecting him to lazily roam the pasture but instead noticed that he seemed stationary. The more she looked, the more she became concerned.

After an hour or so, Betty's curiosity peaked, and she walked into the pasture. There was King standing alongside the barbed wire fence, his hind hoof squarely in the middle of tangled barbed wire. To his credit, he had decided not to move the hoof and cause injury. Instead, the smart fellow decided to wait for Betty to extract him from the dangerous wire.

Hillside Lorton Legend, the champion Clydesdale owned by Shona and John Zawadzki, decided he disliked the electric fence that prevented him from opening the

The playful Clydesdale

pasture gate. "He tried every way possible to turn it off," Shona recalls. "He pushed a piece of wood on it, threw dung on top of it, anything to short circuit the gate."

After Shona and her husband John returned home from a social event a kilometer from the legendary town of Lesmahagow, Scotland, Shona noticed a round, plump rump sticking out from the covered hall between the entrance to the home and barn area. Closer inspection revealed that one of their Clydesdales had decided she wanted to pay a visit to the kitchen area, but had gotten stuck in the narrow hall. "But she then just waited patiently for us to come home," Shona said. "I thought I detected a bit of a grin on her face when we caught her red-handed."

When Clydesdale owners Tom and Cheryl Kenyon of Blossom Valley Clydesdales farm in Nashville, Indiana realized they had an orphan foal, they named Blossom Valley Maguin, they wondered how the little filly would make it through the early years all alone. Quick thinking caused them to purchase Gretta, a two-month-old pygmy goat. Unlike the goat tossed from the stall into the air in the film Seabiscuit, this foal and the goat became fast friends. Tom and Cheryl love to watch them play and they are certain the foal would have died if not for Gretta. Each day the goat wanders the pastures with all of the Clydesdales, but every night she and the filly sleep together in their stall in the barn.

For years, Budweiser housed hundreds of goats at Grant's Farm in St. Louis. Watching over them for several years was Annabelle Farrell, wife of Barry. "He was the horse man and I was the goat woman," she says.

Annabelle recalls another animal taking a liking to the Clydesdales during her years at Grant's Farm. "There was a big red banty rooster who scampered out of the barn every morning," she recalls. "It then headed for the corral where it would jump up on the back of certain Clydesdales and then stay there proud as could be as the Clyde wandered around the pasture. The Clydes would try to shake that rooster off, but they couldn't do it. How that rooster loved to ride around."

Blossom Valley Maguin and her pal Gretta, the goat

Kids in youth classes pose with a Clydesdale at the 2003 National Show

Speaking of companionship, Michelle Whitesel of Germantown, Ohio became concerned when her two-year-old mare Cissy wouldn't trust anyone. This continued even after the horse was broken. Michelle didn't know what to do until one day her seven-year-old daughter Rebecca walked into the barn and climbed up on Cissy's railing. The youngster called the distrustful mare over and, to Michelle's surprise, Cissy laid her head on Rebecca's shoulder. From that day to this, Cissy has been a trusting horse even though Michelle doesn't exactly know why.

Carl Probst stands in front of Vintage carriages at Grant's Farm in St. Louis

Carl Probst, a horse handler at Grant's Farm in St. Louis for twelve years, interacts with Clydesdales every day. "I talk to them," he says, "and even though they don't talk back, they know what is going on. When I do something dumb, they just look at me like 'why did you do that?'"

Probst says the Clydesdales are very sociable. "They will walk over and see what is going on," he says. "They want to know what you are doing." He is also amazed at the horse's reaction to children, especially those that are blind or handicapped. "One of those kids can poke them in the eye or pinch them and the Clyde won't react since they seem to sense the disability in the child. If I did that, they would be upset. At the Shriner's Hospital, the older Clydes we took would play with those kids, poking their heads down in the covers and having fun. They will also put their heads down to the kid's level so they can be petted."

Ned Niemiec echoes Carl Probst's thoughts that Clydesdales are keenly aware of what is going on around them. "I can tell when they understand what I am saying," he says. "They will nod or move their head or nudge me to let me know."

Niemiec says the belief that Clydesdales don't pay attention is false. "They may appear to be nonchalant about things, but when a new horse is brought into the stall area, their ears perk up and they move to the front of their stalls. It's like they have radar checking out who the new horse is."

"Loyalty is also a wonderful trait of Clydesdales," Niemiec says. "We had a horse die in the pasture," he recalls. "And his two buddies wouldn't leave that spot, wouldn't come into the barn. We had to go get them."

Ned has never spied his Clydesdales tempted with alcoholic beverages, but legend has it that one Clydesdale favored the barley in beer. He is alleged to have spied a beer can sitting on a fence post and then tipped it up to taste the brew. No word on any tests for intoxication!

When a Scottish groom became too inebriated to accompany his Clydesdale home, the horse went on its way. Apparently feeling a bit bad on the groom's condition, it returned, whinnied, woke up the groom, positioned its tail so the groom could grab on, and pulled the groom to the safety of its barn.

Alcohol was not the cause of one Clydesdale's disappointment with the hay he was left to eat. Deciding it was too dry, he simply dipped the tasty morsels into a nearby pail to wet it before chomping away. Dr. Martin English, former president of the Clydesdale Breeders of the U.S.A., says he has a mare "that does this with every meal. So did her mother, so does her daughter. We call it 'making tea.'"

Clydesdale owners are quite the practical jokers and one prank played on a fellow owner is legend. To protect the guilty, names cannot be used, but suffice it to say that when an owner drove for more than two days straight to arrive at a show, he was quite tired. A few beers sealed his fate, and he collapsed in a stall dead asleep. Seizing the opportunity, a couple of his buddies removed his trousers and painted his private parts purple, his favorite color. Only when he decided to go to the bathroom after awaking did they hear a holler as the owner discovered his fate.

Young Logan Behn tends to his favorite Clydesdale

At the National Clydesdale Show in Waterloo, Iowa in the 1970s, Jim Emmons was a conspirator with Dan Jones in causing one exhibitor to think twice about racing into his tent without hesitation.

This tale began when Emmons and Jones hid a man's wagon in a nearby tent. When he returned, he scratched his head wondering where his wagon was. He searched for three hours even though the wagon had only been moved about thirty feet. Jim and company finally clued him in, but only after the poor exhibitor ran into his tent through the flap to avoid the rain and flattened his nose when he banged into the wagon.

No damaged nose was involved in this story, but leave a gate open and the Clydesdale will make a run, or rather trot for it. Grace, owned by the Jerry Wismer family, decided to pay a Saturday night call on a neighbor down the road. When she arrived there, she simply stood in the yard, and then made a circle back to the Wismers'. "Some people believe Clydesdales aren't fast," Barbara recalls. "But they are and you can't chase them down. They will stay just far enough ahead that you can't reach them. They are creatures of habit and will return to their stalls or barn eventually. Grace certainly did."

Ben, a Budweiser hitch horse retired to Great American Clydesdales, gained quite a reputation for his appetite. After it was discovered that he had a liking for peppermint candy, a nearby grocery store collected all of its leftover Christmas candy and gave it to Ben for future use. He also fancied sugary donuts, grabbing them out of Mike Collins's hand while he was talking with a guest. As Ben aged (he lived twenty-four years), his head hung low and he walked slowly as he moped along when he left the stall for the paddock, but when it was time to return at dinner, it was a different story. His gait became a trot, and he was lively and bouncy as he headed for the stall. Most times, no lead rope was even required as Ben darted toward his evening meal.

Clydesdale mare (Linda) pulls Santa (Don Vekas) through their neighborhood delivering kids to an annual hot chocolate and Christmas cookie party

Ah, the Buddy System

No eating was involved, but one Scottish breeder was so convinced that if he let a Clydesdale mare see the white markings of a stallion this would in turn produce those same markings. He therefore blindfolded the mare until service was performed and swore it worked every time.

Triplets and twin Clydesdales have been spotted. In one instance, the foal looked like neither the mare nor the stallion but suspiciously like the pony the groom rode to match the two Clydesdales.

Even though she has never seen twin or triplet Clydesdales, Krista Cranston of Cranston Farms in Canada discovered a use for Clydesdales no one had considered. If she rubs Mac a bit, he will return the favor by taking his nose and rubbing it across her back. She calls it a "nibble massage."

Naming a Clydesdale is quite enjoyable, and many imaginative ones have been used. Breeder Sharon Priebe says she named Boots, Scoot, 'N Boogie such because "just out of the sack, she was running to mom hungry." Ronnie Wismer recalls choosing Cedar Lane Hurricane because "the horse just came raring out of the stall."

Mary Q. Flinn, along with her husband David, owners of Starlane Farms in Lansing, New York says her Clydesdale Eleanor was so named because of her elegance. Another was Snowdrop, born early and white, and another Lily, in celebration of Good Friday, her birthday. Mouthy Mavis was so named because she "talked" so much, and Pooh after Winnie the Pooh.

Great American Clydesdales chooses their names based on patriotic Americans. Among them are Benjamin Franklin, Abe Lincoln, Dolly Madison, and Abigail Adams. Another owner uses the names of rock and roll stars including Elvis. No word on whether he can wiggle like the King used to.

Typical Show Wagons

Ken Airgood competes at the 2004 Columbus Carriage Classic Show

The World's Most Magical Horse

Other amusing names are Rock & Roll Popeye, Battle River Ernie, and Tall Tree's Glen. A favorite is Tablerock's Zeus Ontha Loose, causing one to wonder if this Clydesdale is roaming the countryside looking to conquer the world.

Regardless of the name, the Clydesdale is a special breed like no other. Skeptics only have to watch the twinkle in the horse's eyes when they are nudging a child, proudly pulling a six horse hitch, or parading in a show ring with feather flying in the breeze. Whether they are simply a beloved pet, a devoted workhorse, or a champion of the world, the Clydesdale is the grandest of the grand, truly the world's most magical horse.

> ### Where may I learn more about Clydesdales?
>
> Most current owners would welcome the opportunity to visit and answer questions. During the summer and fall, many Clydesdales compete at state and county fairs. This is a wonderful opportunity to observe and learn.

Marty and David Soukup of Diamond S Clydesdales, compete in the unicorn at the 2004 Elcorn County Fair

Appendix

Lead Team
©C. Marcus Stone www.MarcusStone.com

Clydesdales Store

www.clydesusa.com
or by calling 815.247.8780

Sample Items:
Anheuser Busch Collectable Figurines
Coats, Shirts, and Sweatshirts
Youth Clothing
Hats
Socks
Books and Videos
Cards, Posters, Prints, and Rubber Stamps
Bags and Duffels
Jewelry
Gifts or Miscellaneous Items

Bibliography

Anheuser Busch Historian. *Remembrance of Clydesdales Breeders of the United States Visit To Grant's Farm.* 2004.

Baird, Eric. *The Clydesdale Horse.* London: BT Batsford, Ltd., 1982.

Clydesdale Breeders Association of the U.S.A. *Clydesdale News,* Various Issues.

Coleman, Alix and Steven D. Price. *All The King's Horses, The Story of the Budweiser Clydesdales.* Viking Press, 1983.

Edwards, Elwyn Hartley. *The New Rider's Horse Encyclopedia.* Irvington, New York: Hydra Publishing, 2003.

Edwards, Elwyn Hartley. *Wild Horses, A Spirit Unbroken.* Stillwater, Minnesota: Voyageur Press, 1995.

Flanigan, Karen C. *Those Magnificent Clydesdales, The Gentle Giants.* New York: Crown Publishers, 1977.

MacEwan, Grant. *Heavy Horses, An Illustrated History of the Draft Horse.* Canada: Western Producer Prairie Books, 1986.

Mischka, Robert A. *Draft Horse Images.* Whitewater, Wisconsin: Heart Prairie Press, 1994.

Mischka, Robert A. *It's Showtime, A Beginner's Guide to Showing Draft Horses.* Whitewater, Wisconsin: Heart Prairie Press, 1995.

Price, Steven D. *The Quotable Horse Lover.* Guilford, Connecticut: The Lyons Press, 1999.

Russell, Valerie. *Heavy Horses of the World.* Whitewater, Wisconsin: Heart Prairie Press, 1992.

Telleen, Maury. *The Draft Horse Journal,* Various Issues.

Whitlock, Ralph. *Gentle Giants, The Past, Present, and Future of Heavy Horses.* Cambridge: The Lutterworth Press, 1976.

Zawadzki, John. *The Clydesdale International.* Middleholm Farm, Lanarkshire, Scotland: Various Issues.

Clydesdales Association Contacts

Australia

Commonwealth Horse Society

The Royal Agricultural Society of Australia

Melbourne Showgrounds

Epsom Rod. Ascotvale

Victoria 3032

Telephone: 03.9281.7444

Website: **www.Clydesdalehorse.com**

Email: **cchs@rasv.com.au**

Canada

Clydesdale Horse Association of Canada

Secretary Marlene Langille

RR 2, Hopewell, Nova Scotia, Canada, BOKICO

Telephone: 902.923.2600

Email: **mlangille@awacom.com**

Great Britain and Ireland

Clydesdale Horse Society of Great Britain and Ireland

Marguerite Osborne, SecretaryKinclune, Kingoldrum, Kirriemuir, Angus DD8 5HX, United Kingdom

Website: **www.Clydesdalehorsesociety.com**

Email: **secretary@Clydesdalehorsesociety.com**

Telephone and Fax: 01575 570900

Clydesdales Association Contacts (Cont.)

New Zealand
Clydesdales Horse Society of New Zealand V.L. Simmons

Piako Rd. R.D. 1Hamilton, New Zealand

Telephone and Fax: 0.7.824.3813

South Africa
Contact: Jinny Martin P.O. Box 11

Clarens, Free State, Africa 9707

Telephone: 058.256.1105

Email: **rojin@nnet.co.za**

United States
Clydesdale Breeders of the U.S.A.

17346 Kelley Road, Pecatonica, Illinois, 61603 U.S.A.

Website: **www.Clydesusa.com**

Email: **secretary@Clydesusa.com**

Telephone: 815.247.8780

Fax: 815.249.8337

Acknowledgments

No book is possible without the assistance of many people. This is especially true when the book focuses on a subject, as this one does, that the author knew little about before accepting the assignment.

To my brother Jack and his wife Sue, thank you so much for this opportunity. Without your support, this book would not have been possible.

To Betty Groves, Randy Groves, and Cathy Behn, I say thank you in spades. Each contributed their knowledge and understanding to this project from its outset. Each also possesses a love for Clydesdales that is symbolic of the caring for the animals I witnessed wherever I traveled to learn about them and their origins.

To Jim Emmons, a super thank you for your wisdom and patience with a novice who, before writing this book, didn't know a Clydesdale from a thoroughbred. Your expertise, dedication to accuracy, and superb writings about Clydesdales have been inspiring.

To John and Shona Zawadzki and their daughter Rhonagh, thank you for the hospitality shown me during my visit to the Valley of Clydes in Scotland. Permitting me to share your knowledge and passion for the breed is most appreciated. I also thank John for his outstanding assistance with the accuracy of this book. His knowledge of the history of the Clydesdales is beyond comprehension.

To Dr. Martin English, past president of the Clydesdale Breeders of the U.S.A., thanks for your review of the initial draft of the manuscript. Your insight and recommendations are most appreciated.

To Tom Brewster, many thanks for sharing your Clydesdale heritage with me, and your expertise about judging the wondrous animal. The many photographs you allowed me to see provided visualization of the Clydesdale horse in the olden days.

To Jim Poole, the learned Budweiser Clydesdales guru, thank you for your assistance with providing advice regarding the content of the book. And for making certain of the accuracy of the information regarding August Busch, Jr., and his contributions to the continuation of the breed. Your associates Michelle Russell and Barry Murov along with Anheuser-Busch historian Dr. William Vollmar are also thanked for their respective contributions.

To Richard Wegner for his knowledge of the breed and to Robert A. Mischka for his assistance in providing photographs for the book. I also thank Richard Derrer for his practical knowledge of the Clydesdale horse.

To the Wismer family of Canada: Jerry, Barbara, and Ronnie, who befriended me at the Royal Agricultural Winter Fair in Toronto. By watching them, I learned the true family value of raising Clydesdales.

To Darryl Cobbs for his insight into the Clydesdale breed. He and his family continue the great tradition of Clydesdale owners.

To my loyal compatriot Kelly James, thanks for your research and organizational capabilities. Together, we learned about an animal that neither of us knew much about.

To Nancy Crenshaw for her editing experience, and to Sarah Foster for assisting us with collecting the photographs that appear in this book.

To Allison Anderson, my friend and office assistant, thank you for keeping me organized and focused on the book. You are an invaluable resource.

To Lynne and Mike Liechty, and Stephanie Feeley of Commercial Graphics Company for their printing expertise. The professional layout and printing of this book is due to them.

To my sisters Anne and Debbie for their love and support, and those many members of the Clydesdales family around the world who helped me learn about the wonderful breed so that I did not make a fool of myself writing this book.

To Black Sox, my mischievous black Labrador, thanks for being my friend and companion during the writing process. Your silly antics at five in the morning kept me alert as I composed the text for the book.

And most of all, thank you to the Good Lord for his blessing to write this book about one of His most beautiful creatures. How blessed I am.

— *Mark Shaw*

Clydesdales

The Suffolk Punch will keep the road;
The Percheron goes gay;
The Shire will lean against its load;
All through the longest day;
But where ploughland meets the heather
And earth from sky divides
Through the misty Northern weather,
Stepping two and two together
All fire and feather,
Comes the Clydesdales!

The Hunter gallops on the lea.
The Garron treads the ling.
The Hackney, touching nose and knee,
Will make the roadway ring;
But, apart from play and pleasure,
With the sweat upon their sides,
Where the furrow is to measure,
And the earth to turn for treasure,
Surfs of little leisure
Go the Clydesdales!

To each the favorite of his heart,
To each his chosen breed,
In gig and saddle, plough and cart
To serve his separate need;
Blue blood for him who races.
Clean limbs for him who rides,
But for me the giant graces,
And the white and honest faces
The power upon the traces
Of the Clydesdales!

O. R. Cadian
The Clydesdales Breed
Published by the Clydesdales
Horse Society of Great Britain
& Ireland, 1938

Airgood Acres Spirited Angel and her 2003 stud foal, Airgood Acres Axel owned Ken and Sonja Airgood of Marshall, Wisconsin

Photograph/Illustration Credit List

Front Cover (Main) - Horses owned by Steve and Marcia Haase - Courtesy of Bob Mischka

Front Cover (Small Left) - Horses Plowing thru field Courtesy of Bob Mischka

Front Cover (Small Right) - Shania, a mare, stands watch with Miles, a foal, owned by Jeanne Williams, Woodside, California - Courtesy of Jeanne Williams

Back Cover (Small Left) - Nicholas Wismer and Skipper Courtesy of The Windsor Star

Back Cover (Small Right) - Chuck and Ginger Hansell driving Ben a 16-yr-old roan Clydesdale Courtesy of Bob Mischka

Inside Cover Jacket - Clydesdale Mare C.I.E. Rose and her 2002 foal, NorthStar Rachel. They make their home with Rose and Bob Henderson of Mukwonago, Wisconsin Courtesy of Bob Mischka

Back Inside Cover Jacket - Mark Shaw and Clydesdale Courtesy of Mark Shaw

Sponsored by page - A/B archives

Photograph on Poem page- Courtesy of Needman, Harper and Steers

p. 5 - Courtesy of C. Marcus Stone

p. 7 - Courtesy of Bluffview Clydesdales, Jack and Carol Angelbeck

p. 8 - (Top Right) Courtesy of A/B archives

p. 8 - (Bottom) Courtesy of A/B archives

p. 9 - Courtesy of Kinuko Y. Kraft

p. 10 - Courtesy of Random House Children's Classics

p. 11 - Courtesy of C. Marcus Stone

p. 13 - Courtesy of art.com

p. 14- Courtesy of Mark Shaw

p. 15 - (Top Right) Ballantine Publishing Group

p. 17 - Courtesy of Lisa Banga

p. 20 - Courtesy of Bob Mischka

p. 21 - Courtesy of Studio Cactus

p. 20 - Courtesy of Studio Cactus

p. 21 - Courtesy of dk images

p. 22 - (Top) Courtesy of Studio Cactus

p. 23 - Courtesy of dk images

p. 24 - Courtesy of Bob Mischka

p. 25 - Courtesy of dk images

p. 26 - (Bottom Left) Courtesy of Ned Niemiec

p. 26 - (Top Right) Courtesy of Bob Mischka

p. 27 - Courtesy of Bob Mischka

p. 28 - (Bottom Left) Courtesy of Bob Mischka

p. 29 - Courtesy of Bob Mischka

p. 30 - (Top) Courtesy of Mark Shaw

p. 30 - (Bottom Left) Courtesy of Mark Shaw

p. 31 - (Top) Courtesy of Jim Emmons

p. 31 - (Bottom) Courtesy of Mark Shaw

p. 32 - Courtesy of Lynn Cassels-Caldwell

p. 33 - Courtesy of the Wismer Family

p. 35 - Courtesy of Lisa Banga

p. 36 - Courtesy of Stine

p. 37 - Courtesy of Stine

p. 38 - (Top) Courtesy of Stine

p. 38 - (Bottom Left) Courtesy of Clydesdale Breeders of the USA

p. 39 - Courtesy of Jim Emmons

p. 40 - (Bottom Left) Courtesy of Jim Emmons

p. 40 - (Top Right) Courtesy of Jim Emmons

p. 41 - (Top Right) Courtesy of John Zawadzki

p. 41 - (Bottom Left) Courtesy of Mark Shaw

p. 41 - (Center Left) Courtesy of Mark Shaw

p. 42 - Courtesy of Richard Wegner

p. 43 - Courtesy of Lynn Cassels-Caldwell

p. 45 - Courtesy of Jim Richendollar, Draft Horse Archives

p. 46 - Courtesy of Bob Mischka

p. 47 - Courtesy of Bob Mischka

p. 48 - (Top Left) Courtesy of Bob Mischka

p. 48 - (Right) Courtesy of Bob Mischka

p. 49 - (Top Right) Courtesy of Bob Mischka

p. 49 - (Bottom) Courtesy of Bob Mischka

p. 50 - Courtesy of Jim Richendollar, Draft Horse Archives

p. 51 - Courtesy of Clydesdale News

p. 52 - Courtesy of Jim Richendollar, Draft Horse Archives

p. 53 - Courtesy of Joe Mischka

p. 54 - Courtesy of Jim Emmons

p. 55 - (Top) Courtesy of Draft Horse Journal

p. 55 - (Bottom) Courtesy of Steve Dorfman

p. 56 - (Bottom) Courtesy of Jim Emmoms

p. 56 - (Top) Courtesy of Jim Emmons

p. 57 - Courtesy of Bob Mischka

p. 59 - Courtesy of Bob Mischka

p. 60 - Courtesy of Ned Niemiec

p. 61 - (Bottom) Courtesy of Ned Niemiec

p. 61 - (Top) Courtesy of Ned Niemiec

p. 61 - (Top) Courtesy of Ned Niemiec

p. 62 - (Top) Courtesy A/B archives

p. 62 - (Bottom) Courtesy of A/B archives

p. 63 - Courtesy of Jim Richendollar, Draft Horse Archives

p. 64 - Courtesy of A/B archives

p. 64 - Courtesy of A/B archives

p. 65 - Courtesy of Jim Richendollar, Draft Horse Archives

p. 67 - Courtesy of Mark Shaw

p. 68 - Courtesy of Bob Mischka

p. 69 - (Bottom Left) Courtesy of Draft Horse Journal

p. 69 - (Top Right) Courtesy of Clydesdale News

p. 70 - (Top Right) Courtesy of A/B archives

p. 70 - (Bottom Left) Courtesy of A/B archives

p. 71 - Courtesy of A/B archives

p. 72 - Courtesy of A/B archives

p. 73 - Courtesy of A/B archives

p. 74 - (Bottom Left) Courtesy of Mark Shaw

Photograph/Illustration Credit List

p. 74 - (Top Right) Courtesy of Lynn Cassels-Caldwell
p. 75 - (Bottom) Courtesy of Clydesdale News
p. 75 - (Top) Courtesy of Clydesdale News
p. 76 - (Top Right) Courtesy of Clydesdale News
p. 76 - Courtesy of Mark Shaw
p. 77 - (Top Left) Courtesy of Clydesdale News
p. 77 - (Top Right) Courtesy of Clydesdale News
p. 78 - (Top) Courtesy of Clydesdale News
p. 78 - (Bottom) Courtesy of Michael and Cheri Moleski
p. 79 - Courtesy of Akorn Creations
p. 80 - (Top) Courtesy of Mark Shaw
p. 80 - (Bottom) Courtesy of Mark Shaw
p. 81 - (Left) Courtesy of Betty Groves
p. 81 - (Right) Courtesy of Mark Shaw
p. 82 - Courtesy of the Wismer Family
p. 82 - Courtesy of the Wismer Family
p. 83 - Courtesy of the Wismer Family
p. 84 - Courtesy of Bob Mischka
p. 85 - (Bottom) Courtesy of Jack Shaw
p. 85 - (Top) Courtesy of Jack Shaw
p. 86 - (Left) Courtesy of Mark Shaw
p. 86 - (Right) Courtesy of Brian Richman
p. 87 - Courtesy of Faith Brooks
p. 89 - Courtesy of Clydesdale Breeders of the USA
p. 90 - Courtesy Jeanne Williams
p. 91 - (Left) Courtesy of Brian Richman
p. 91 - (Middle Left) Courtesy of Bob Mischka
p. 91 - (Middle Right) Courtesy of Clydesdale Breeders of the USA
p. 91 - (Right) Courtesy of Clydesdale Breeders of the USA
p. 92 - Courtesy of The Windsor Star
p. 93 - Courtesy of Ron Wismer
p. 94 - (Bottom) Courtesy of Mark Shaw
p. 94 - (Top) Courtesy of Mark Shaw
p. 95 - Courtesy of Lynne Liechty
p. 96 - Courtesy of Lynn Cassels-Caldwell
p. 97 - Courtesy of Bob Mischka
p. 98 - Courtesy of Linda Sioux Stenson
p. 99 - (Top) Courtesy of Lynn Cassels-Caldwell
p. 99 - (Bottom) Courtesy of Lynn Cassels-Caldwell
p. 100 - (Top) Courtesy of Mark Shaw
p. 100 - (Bottom) Courtesy of Mark Shaw
p. 101 - (Bottom Left) Courtesy of Mark Shaw
p. 101 - (Top Right) Courtesy of Clydesdale Breeders of the USA
p. 102 - (Top Left) Courtesy of Mark Shaw
p. 102 - (Top Right) Courtesy of Mark Shaw
p. 102 - (Middle Left) Courtesy of Jack Shaw
p. 102 - (Middle Right) Courtesy of Clydesdale Breeders of the USA
p. 102 - (Bottom) Courtesy of Janice Rasmussen

p. 103 - Courtesy of Clydesdale Breeders of the USA
p. 105 - Courtesy of Lynn Cassels-Caldwell
p. 106 - (Bottom Left) Toronto Royal Agricultural Winter Fair
p. 106 - (Top) Courtesy of Great American Clydesdales
p. 107 - Courtesy of Bob Mischka
p. 108 - Courtesy of Ned Niemiec
p. 109 - Courtesy of Bob Mischka
p. 110 - (Bottom Left) Courtesy of Mark Shaw
p. 110 - (Top Right) Courtesy of Brian Richman
p. 111 - (Bottom) Courtesy of Mark Shaw
p. 111 - (Top Right) Courtesy of Lynn Cassels-Caldwell
p. 112 - Courtesy if Big Ed's Photos
p. 113 - Courtesy of Brian Richman
p. 115 - Courtesy of Bob Mischka
p. 117 - Courtesy of Lisa Banga
p. 118 - Courtesy of Tony Knecht Castagnasso, Mission Bell Clydesdales
p. 119 - (Top Right) Courtesy of Tom Kenyon
p. 120 - (Top) Courtesy of Clydesdale Breeders of the USA
p. 120 - (Bottom) Courtesy of Mark Shaw
p. 121 - Courtesy of Kathy Behn
p. 122 - Courtesy of Jackie Vekas
p. 123 - Courtesy of Betty Groves/Cathy Behn
p. 124 - Courtesy of Casey McBride
p. 125 - Courtesy of Bon Mischka
p. 126 - Courtesy of Bob Mischka
p. 127 - Courtesy of C. Marcus Stone
p. 137 - Courtesy of Bob Mischka
p. 138 - Courtesy of Lisa Banga

The late Bill Muir, Didsbury, Alberta, Canada